759.13
OKE

SANTA CRUZ CITY-COUNTY

D0576689

759.13   Udall, Sharyn
UDA   Rohlfsen.

       O'Keeffe and Texas.

DATE			

SANTA CRUZ PUBLIC LIBRARY
Santa Cruz California

BAKER & TAYLOR

O'Keeffe and Texas

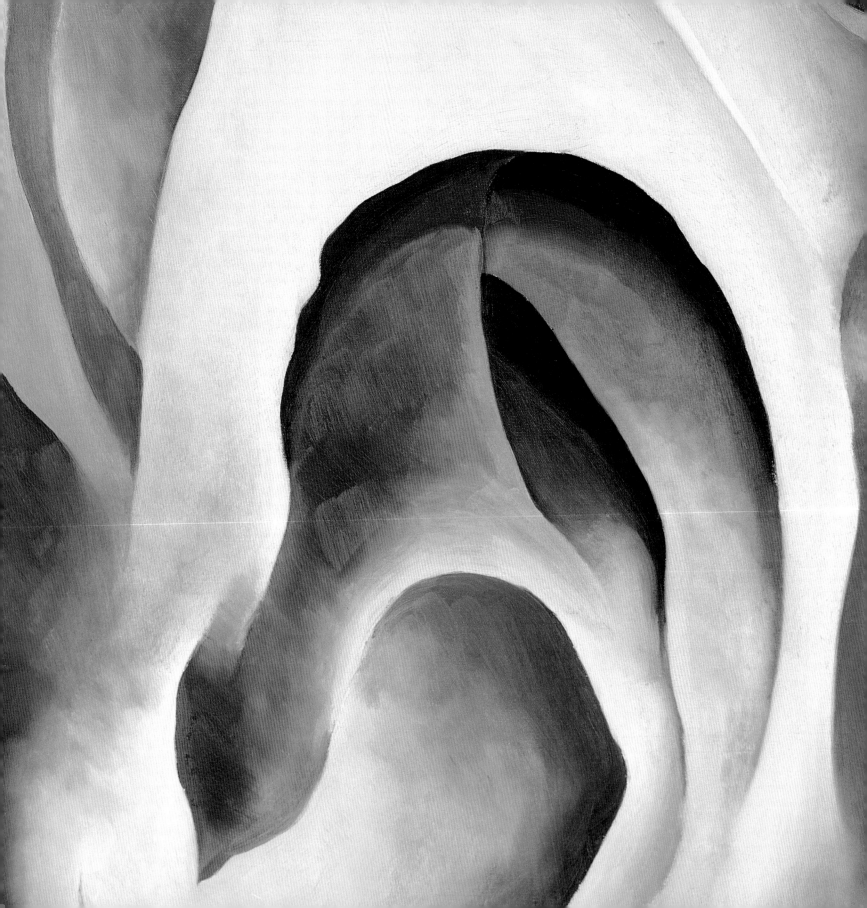

O'Keeffe and Texas

Sharyn R. Udall

TheMcNay

The Marion Koogler McNay Art Museum

in association with Harry N. Abrams, Inc., Publishers

SANTA CRUZ PUBLIC LIBRARY
Santa Cruz California

This book is published to coincide with the exhibition *O'Keeffe and Texas* held at The Marion Koogler McNay Art Museum, in San Antonio, from January 27 to April 5, 1998.

Major funding for this catalogue was provided by the Horse Creek Trust.

Lead funding for this exhibition was provided by the Russell Hill Rogers Fund for the Arts, with additional support from the Marcia and Otto Koehler Foundation, NationsBank Trustee; the Nathalie and Gladys Dalkowitz Foundation, NationsBank Trustee; and from the Elizabeth Huth Coates Exhibition Endowment.

Copyright © 1998 by The Marion Koogler McNay Art Museum

Certain illustrations are covered by claims to copyright cited in the Photograph Credits, page 119.

All rights reserved. No part of this publication may be reproduced, stored in a retrieval system, or transmitted in any form or by any means, electronic, mechanical, photocopying, or otherwise, without prior written permission from the publisher, except by a reviewer who wishes to quote brief passages in connection with a review written for inclusion in a magazine, newspaper, or broadcast.

The Marion Koogler McNay Art Museum
6000 North New Braunfels
P.O. Box 6069
San Antonio, Texas 78209-0069

Distributed in 1998 by Harry N. Abrams, Incorporated, New York

Front cover: *Evening Star, No. V,* 1917 (cat. 17)
Back cover: Alfred Stieglitz, *Georgia O'Keeffe: A Portrait* (fig. 7)
Frontispiece: Detail of *Leaf Motif #2,* 1924 (cat. 37)

Library of Congress Cataloging-in-Publication Data
Udall, Sharyn Rohlfsen.
    O'Keeffe and Texas / Sharyn R. Udall.
       p.   cm.
    Catalogue of an exhibition held at the Marion Koogler McNay Art Museum, in San Antonio.
    ISBN 0-8109-6356-6 (Abrams : alk. paper). —
ISBN 0-916677-39-7 (pbk. : alk. paper)
    1. O'Keeffe, Georgia, 1887–1986—Exhibitions.
  I. Marion Koogler McNay Art Museum. II. Title.
N6537.039A4 1998
759.13—dc21   97-31801

Printed in Hong Kong

Contents

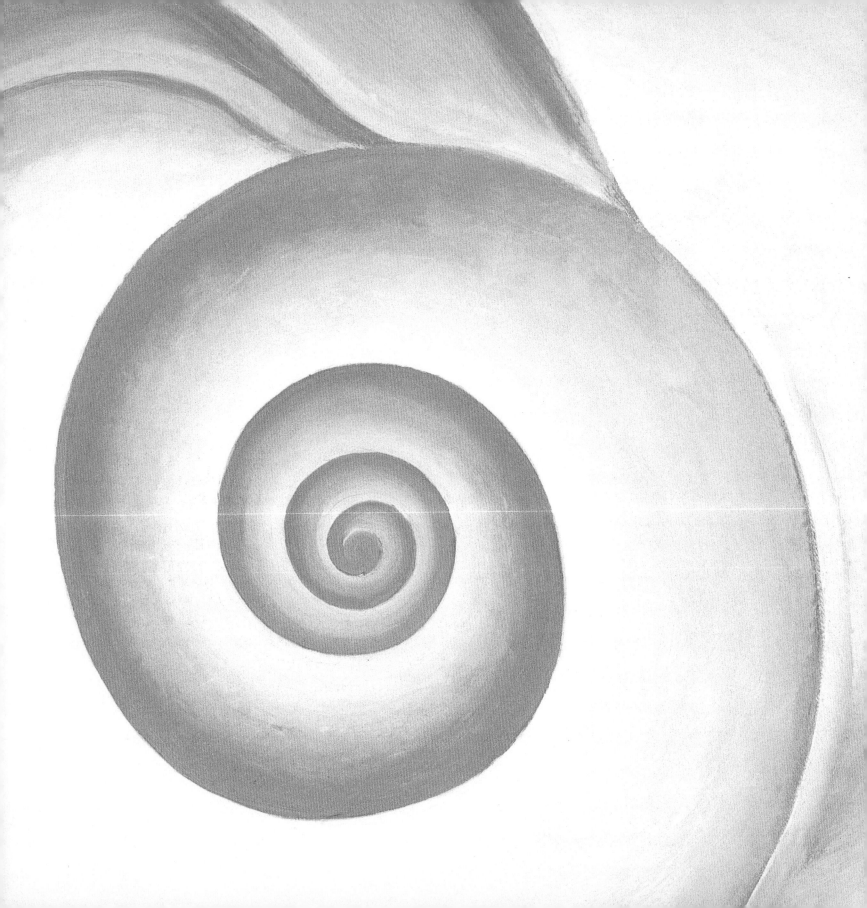

Foreword

In March of 1986, Juan Hamilton hiked Pedernal Mountain and tossed Georgia O'Keeffe's ashes into a strong wind, scattering them into the New Mexico countryside she loved and called her home. The resonance that the spaces of the West had for O'Keeffe was a definitive force in her life and was important to her in death as well. The illuminating essay that Sharyn Udall has written to accompany the exhibition *O'Keeffe and Texas* demonstrates the connection between O'Keeffe and the spirit of place; between her essential self and the vast plains of West Texas.

As a young art student in New York, O'Keeffe heard the theory that the individual's moods were reflected in nature. Variations of the idea—that nature was a solace and source of inspiration—were natural for her to adopt. By the time a twenty-four-year-old Georgia O'Keeffe came to Texas as an art teacher in 1912, she had already begun to use the land as a metaphor for her emotions. Roxana Robinson explains: ". . . the landscape had been

a perennial source of nourishment, a metaphorical restorative, reliable, soothing, necessary . . ."[1]

In the spring of 1918, when O'Keeffe went to see her future husband, Alfred Stieglitz, in New York, she wanted to explain to him in person that the city didn't suit her as a place to live. She had already written Stieglitz that Texas was "a wonderful place—I wonder why everyone doesn't live here."[2] O'Keeffe began a long life of shuttling between the open spaces of the West and the intellectual excitement of the East.

As Udall points out, the redemptive quality of the American landscape had been a staple subject for nineteenth-century American artists like Thomas Moran, Frederick Church, and Albert Bierstadt. Their work was concentrated on the land, marked by trees, rivers, and mountains, not on the sky —but the immensity of the sky was inescapable in West Texas.

The lack of visual limits, which O'Keeffe called the "bigness," is sometimes frightening to people, but was

Detail of *Red Hills with White Shell,* 1938 (cat. 41)

exciting to O'Keeffe. The dry, flat plains of Texas were like an ocean to her. Her spirit began to explore the landscape as she explored herself. In this landscape, there were none of the traditional points of reference. It was a landscape without beginning and end, a chartless space, exhilarating and challenging to her soul. The endless and stark horizons of Texas required O'Keeffe to explore, to extend, to observe . . .

As Sharyn Udall explains, O'Keeffe followed the anti-realist lead of her teacher Arthur Dow, and found in nature the possibility for both formal invention and personal expression. Dow freed her of the need to represent three-dimensional space, allowing her to re-order and use space to express herself. This sort of freedom places a great obligation on the artist to be able to bear public scrutiny. The artist, rather than an established myth, allegory, or idealized landscape, is the subject. Paintings hang in galleries as works of art and personal statements of self.

In 1912 Georgia O'Keeffe was a strong and talented young woman. She was ready for a pilgrimage into herself and the spaces she found there. The landscape of Texas provided a physical manifestation of that inner place and a terrain in which she could mature as an artist.

Ellen Bradbury

Notes
1. Roxana Robinson, *Georgia O'Keeffe: A Life* (New York: Harper and Row, 1989), 155.
2. O'Keeffe, letter to Alfred Stieglitz, 19 April 1918, published in Anita Pollitzer, *A Woman on Paper*, 159.

Acknowledgments

Many individuals and institutions have contributed to the realization of this exhibition. Foremost among them I would like to thank the staff of the McNay Art Museum, every one of whom contributes in some way to the presentation of such a major loan exhibition. I am grateful to all for their good work.

Special thanks are given to Linda Hardberger, Chief Curator, and Heather Lammers, Collections Manager, for their respective assistance in the conceptualization and organization of this exhibition. My thanks also to Rose Glennon, Curator of Education, for her work forming the accompanying educational programs for the exhibition and for her editorial assistance. Thanks are also due to Sandi Goldsmith, Secretary to the Director; Heather Snow, Tobin Collection Assistant; Steve Bennett, former Public Relations Officer; Ellen Batt, Special Events Coordinator; Dianne Powell and Marti Alpard, Development Directors over the life of the project; Edward J. Hepner, Chief Preparator, and Patric Cormier, Assistant Preparator; and Ann Jones, Librarian.

The guest curator wishes to acknowledge the assistance of the following individuals for their help with her research for the exhibition: William de Buys; Stephanie Gaskins of the Ipswich Historical Society, Massachusetts; Stuart Ashman, Director, and Joseph Traugott of the Museum of Fine Arts, Museum of New Mexico; Sarah Greenough, Curator of Photographs, National Gallery of Art; Barbara Buhler Lynes, Director of the Georgia O'Keeffe Catalogue Raisonné Project; Elizabeth Glassman, Director, and Sarah Burt and Judy Lopez of The Georgia O'Keeffe Foundation; Juan Hamilton; Gerald Peters and Catherine Whitney of The Gerald Peters Gallery; Dean Porter, Director, Snite Museum of Art, University of Notre Dame; Anthony Montoya of the Paul Strand Archive; Stewart Udall; Tom Veilleux Gallery, Farmington, Maine; and Donald Gallup of the Yale Collection of American Literature, Beinecke Library, Yale University.

The organizing curator wishes to thank the following individuals and institutions for their generous loans and for their assistance with loan arrangements or the preparation of this publication: Jock Reynolds, Director, and Denise Johnson of the Addison Gallery of American Art, Phillips Academy; James C. Moore, Director, Ellen Landes, Tom Lark, and Marilee Schmit Nason of the Albuquerque Museum; Patrick McCracken, Director, and Jackie Smith of the Amarillo Museum of Art; Rick Stewart, Director, Jane Meyers, Melissa Thompson, and Courtney De Angelis of the Amon Carter Museum; James Wood, Director, Jeremy Strick, and Mary Malhern of the Art Institute of Chicago; Robert P. Bergman, Director, Tom E. Hinson, and Mary Suzor of The Cleveland Museum of Art; David Turner, Director, and Kathy Reynolds of the Colorado Springs Fine Arts Center; David Levy, Director, Jack Cowart, and Kirsten Verdi of the Corcoran Gallery of Art; John Vanausdall, Director, and Bob Tucker

of the Eiteljorg Museum of American Indians and Western Art; William U. Eiland, Director, Lynn Perdue, and Annelies Mondi of the Georgia Museum of Art; Bret Waller, Director, Ellen Lee, Terry Harley-Wilson, and Ruth V. Roberts of the Indianapolis Museum of Art; Dana Self, Curator, and Dawn Giegerich of the Kemper Museum of Contemporary Art & Design; Susan Davidson, Associate Curator, and Julia Bakke of the Menil Collection; Philippe de Montebello, Director, Ida Balboul, Marceline McKee, and Deanna Cross of the Metropolitan Museum of Art; Russell Bowman, Director, Leigh Albritton, and Judith Palmese of the Milwaukee Museum of Art; Peter Marzio, Director, and Linda Wilhelm of the Museum of Fine Arts, Houston; Stuart Ashman, Director, and Joan Tafoya of the Museum of Fine Arts, Museum of New Mexico; Cora Rosevear, Department of Painting and Sculpture, Thomas D. Grischkowsky, and Anna Hillen of the Museum of Modern Art; Earl A. Powell, Director, Lisa Mariam, and

Sara Sanders-Buell of the National Gallery of Art; Shirley Thompson, Director, and Fouad Kanaan of the National Gallery of Canada; Elizabeth Broun, Director, and Abigail Terrones of the National Museum of American Art, Smithsonian Institution; Elizabeth Glassman, Director, and Judy Lopez of The Georgia O'Keeffe Foundation; Peter Hassrick, former Director, and Lynn Brittner-Hutton of the Georgia O'Keeffe Museum; Barbara and James Palmer; Michael Grauer, Director, and Mary Moore of the Panhandle Plains Historical Museum, West Texas A & M University; Gerald Peters, Director, Catherine Whitney, and Murfy Nix of the Gerald Peters Gallery; Anne d'Harnoncourt, Director, Ann Temkin, and Nancy Wulbrecht of the Philadelphia Museum of Art; Charles Moffett, Director, Joe Holbach, and Lisa Zarrow of the Phillips Collection; James Ballinger, Director, and Heather Northway of the Phoenix Art Museum; James D. Burke, Director, Sidney Goldstein, and Diane Vandegrift of the Saint Louis Art Museum; Dean

Porter, Director, and Robert Smogor of the Snite Museum of Art, University of Notre Dame; Andrea Norris, Director, Janet Dreiling, and Carol Lattuca of the Spencer Museum of Art, the University of Kansas; and Robert L. B. Tobin and Arnold Swartz of the Tobin Foundation.

This exhibition would not have been possible without the lead financial support of the Russell Hill Rogers Fund for the Arts. Their generous and early funding allowed a timely start to this project. Generous financial assistance has also been provided by the Horse Creek Trust; the Marcia and Otto Koehler Foundation, NationsBank Trustee; and by the Nathalie and Gladys Dalkowitz Foundation, NationsBank Trustee. The McNay's Elizabeth Huth Coates Exhibition Endowment has provided additional support. The McNay is deeply grateful to all for their generosity.

My thanks to Ellen Bradbury, Director of the Recursos de Santa Fe, for her insightful foreword to this catalogue. And, most of all, thanks to

Sharyn R. Udall, guest curator, for her excellent work in shaping the exhibition and for her perceptive and graceful essay, which sheds new light on O'Keeffe's work.

William J. Chiego
Director and Organizing Curator

Introduction

Considering that Georgia O'Keeffe has become so powerfully identified with her adopted state of New Mexico, the organization of an exhibition on the theme of O'Keeffe and Texas may be surprising to many. It is still little known today among the broad public that O'Keeffe's first experience of the great spaces of the Southwest took place in the Texas Panhandle, where she went to teach art in 1912, first in Amarillo and then in Canyon, and where she remained until her move to New York in 1918.

It was from this experience that O'Keeffe developed an abiding love and fierce attachment to this distinctive part of the country. It resulted in her annual pilgrimages there from the East by the late 1920s, and her permanent move to New Mexico in 1949, after the death of her husband and mentor, Alfred Stieglitz.

Knowledge of this crucial early period has begun to grow, and it is the purpose of this exhibition to demonstrate how many of O'Keeffe's fundamental pictorial concepts were first established during these Texas years. The works she executed in Texas and those created during the subsequent decades show the resilience and longevity of certain key compositional themes and concepts of form and color that remained vital for her for over half a century, until she effectively ceased painting in the early 1970s.

The organization of this exhibition exploring the importance of Texas to O'Keeffe's career is especially meaningful for the McNay Art Museum. Founded in 1950 as the state's first museum of modern art, the McNay has developed particular strength in the work of the American modernists of the Stieglitz circle, including O'Keeffe, John Marin, Marsden Hartley, and Arthur Dove. Museum founder Marion Koogler McNay formed the foundation for this aspect of the collection with her acquisition of many contemporary American watercolors and drawings during the 1930s and 1940s. Her acquisitions were augmented by subsequent bequests and gifts of modern American paintings, especially those of Mary and Sylvan Lang, Helen Miller Jones, and Robert L. B. Tobin, as well as by important purchases.

This exhibition evolved into its present form by focusing our investigation on two particular works in the Museum's collection: the 1917 watercolor *Evening Star, No. V,* which O'Keeffe painted during her Texas years, and the 1953 oil *From the Plains I,* a reminiscence of the Texas Panhandle painted some four decades later. In a sense, this exhibition was motivated by a series of questions. Why was O'Keeffe moved to paint a remembrance of Texas so many years later? What was the significance of the Texas Pan-handle's hold on her imagination? Why did she call Texas her spiritual home?

It is our goal to answer these questions by bringing together the works in this exhibition and by examining the significance of her Texas years to O'Keeffe's career. Guest curator Sharyn Udall has provided a structure for this exhibition and for her catalogue essay that offers a fresh approach to O'Keeffe's work. It is especially revealing of O'Keeffe's strong tendency toward abstraction and the dialogue she conducted between representation and non-representation throughout her career. We hope it will provide a better understanding of the maturation of O'Keeffe's particular vision during her Texas years, and a fuller appreciation of the character of her work.

William J. Chiego
Director

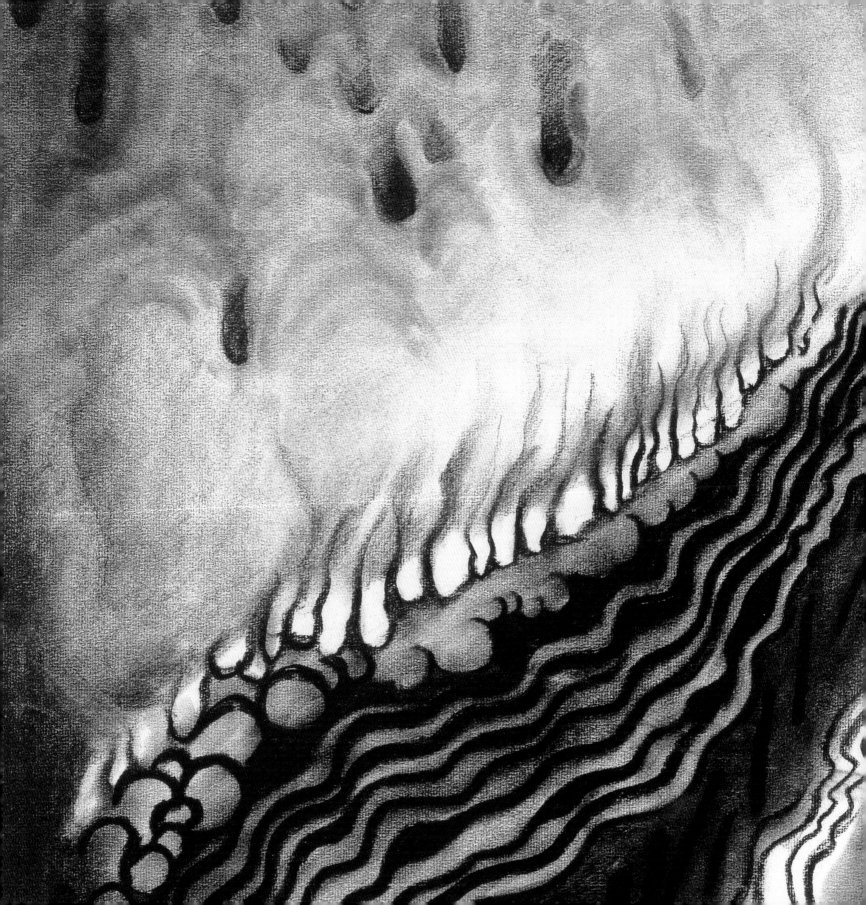

Sharyn R. Udall

O'Keeffe and Texas

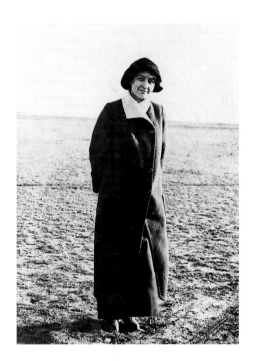

Figure 1
Georgia O'Keeffe in Amarillo ca. 1912
Silver gelatin print
Courtesy of The Georgia O'Keeffe
Foundation

Left: Detail of *Special No. 9*, 1915 (cat. 2)

* Georgia O'Keeffe's life has been docu-
mented exhaustively in many publications. For a summary of her biography,
the reader is referred to the Chronology
included in this catalogue (pp. 107–12)
or to the several full-length biographies
listed in the notes following this essay.

Texas existed in Georgia O'Keeffe's
imagination long before she saw it
with her own eyes. As children,
O'Keeffe and her siblings listened
raptly while their mother read them
tales of life in the Wild West. Many
years later, when Georgia was offered
a position teaching art in the Amarillo
public schools, she jumped at the
chance: "I was hugely excited about
going to Texas, because of all those
stories that Mother had read to us.
Texas was the great place in the world
as far as I was concerned."[1]

So strongly was O'Keeffe drawn to
Texas that she spent a good portion of
a decade there: in Amarillo from 1912
to 1914; then in Canyon for another
teaching position at West Texas State
Normal College, from 1916 to 1918.*
Stepping off the train at Amarillo in
1912, twenty-four-year-old O'Keeffe
found herself in a place unlike any she
had ever seen. Her mother's stories
of frontier life might have readied her
for the vestiges of cowboy life still in

evidence, but nothing had prepared
her for the place itself.

On the plains of the Panhandle,
distance, space, and isolation were
abundant; noise, crowds, and visual
obstructions were few. The plow had
not yet textured the plains with human
presence. Mostly the land opened out
from one's feet in uninterrupted pro-
gression toward the horizon. And the
wind blew. A few years later O'Keeffe
recalled how she loved Amarillo: "the
wind blows like mad—and there is
nothing after the last house of town
as far as you can see—there is something wonderful about the bigness and
the lonelyness and the windyness of
it all" (fig. 1).[2]

Soon O'Keeffe began to explore
the area on early morning walks, a
habit she had formed while living in
Virginia. She returned windblown, her
clothes coated with dust. "Sometimes
when I came back from walking," she
recalled, "I would be the color of
the road."[3] Most of those roads were

dead-straight, and so were the railroad tracks, the lifeline of the town. Major rail lines intersected at Amarillo and brought it prosperity as a cattle-shipping center.

When she headed south and west from town on her walks, O'Keeffe glimpsed the vast Llano Estacado stretching unbroken as far as the eye could see. Its name, meaning "staked plain," recalls the early Spanish presence in the area, confirmed by recent archaeological findings demonstrating that Coronado's party camped in Blanco Canyon in 1541. That history lay lightly on the land; it was the region's ancient, geological past that left its imprint on the austere Panhandle terrain O'Keeffe came to love.

Within human memory the Great Plains has been a place of almost unrelieved emptiness. But where the West Texas Panhandle now stretches flat and dry, scientists know that there was once a mighty rushing river.[4] It flowed from monsoon-drenched mountains some 225 million years ago, when much of the globe was covered by a supercontinent known as Pangaea. As the chief drainage system of western Pangaea, the river crossed now-arid portions of Texas, New Mexico, Arizona, and Utah, eventually emptying into a sea somewhere in the region of

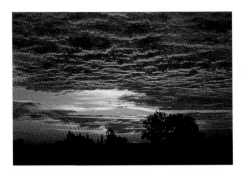

Figure 2
Wyman Meinzer
Sunset, Rolling Plains, Texas
Color transparency

modern Nevada. When the continent of Pangaea broke up, the folding of continental rock and the erosion of mountains eventually diverted Texas rivers into the Gulf. But left behind, strewn along the path of the ancient waters, were rocks and minerals whose age now helps scientists to map the geography of an ancient past.

Georgia O'Keeffe could have known nothing of the scale and force of those primordial geologic events. Nevertheless, the region's topographical severity, suggestive of cataclysmic origins, was very much to her reductivist taste. In the Panhandle she learned to look hard at the limitless earth and sky; in later years, wherever else she went in the West, O'Keeffe sought out signs in the land that pointed to its ancient beginnings.

Despite the scarcity of water on the vast Texas plains, O'Keeffe linked their expanse in her mind—probably unknowingly—with the ancient sea that had once covered the land. In 1916 she said the Texas plains were "more like the ocean than anything else I know—"[5] And nearly a half-century later the impression remained: "Texas," she said, "is the same big wonderful thing that oceans and the highest mountains are."[6] Bigness, yes, but why the repeated association with watery expanses?

The scarcity of water in the Texas Panhandle was new to O'Keeffe, who had grown up in verdant places like Wisconsin and Virginia. West Texas was the first dry place she had lived, and she discovered new ways to think about its arid expanses. When she likened it to a vast sea, it was in part due to her own direct sensory impressions. She noted the wondrous visual events produced by mirages: ". . . mirages people [the landscape] with all sorts of things at times—sometimes Ive seen the most wonderful sunsets over what seemed to be the ocean.—It is great—"[7] (fig. 2).

Generations of earlier travelers to the West had seen it similarly. In a letter to the king of Spain, Coronado described the Llano Estacado as "plains, with no more landmarks than as if we had been swallowed up by the sea . . . because there was not a stone nor a bit of rising ground, nor a tree, nor a shrub, nor anything to go by."[8] Topographical artist Heinrich Balduin Möllhausen passed through West Texas in the 1850s and likened the Llano Estacado to a "vast slumbering Leviathan."[9]

The absence or presence of water has been a critical feature of landscape painting for hundreds of years. Painters of American scenery had long believed water an essential ingredient in their work. Thomas Cole, in his day the nation's premier landscape painter, was adamant: "Without water," declared Cole, "every landscape is defective."[10] His successors agreed in overwhelming numbers. They painted coastlines, rivers, cataracts, ponds—even, in the case of Albert Bierstadt and Thomas Moran, water in the form of ice and snow on mountain peaks.

There were, in fact, few artistic precedents for American landscapes without water. Bodies of water provided the artist with opportunities to suggest movement in time and space and access to a geographic or mythic beyond. Lakes and rivers mirrored nature's moods, whether tranquil or turbulent. They added aspects of monumentality to ordinary scenes. With the weight of so much artistic history and symbolism riding on water, painters such as Möllhausen and O'Keeffe, however unconsciously, may have resorted to watery references from their visual memories to encompass the vast, open expanses of West Texas.

For artists working on the dry plains, the question came down to this: in a land where water—as well as mountains and trees, the nineteenth-century landscape painter's other two staple components—was in short supply, how could the artist create monumental landscape paintings? How suggest transcendence in native scenery? Could the raw materials of the plains—sky, earth, sun, and wind—challenge the artist to make new meaning of its spareness?

Georgia O'Keeffe was uniquely equipped to take on that challenge. She already knew something about the intimate relationship of people to the environment they inhabit: "Where I come from," she said, "the earth means everything. Life depends on it."[11] But O'Keeffe did not find a way to express that dependence until she painted in the West. In Texas came her first realization that artistic expression could grow out of intimacy with place.

O'Keeffe had, unknowingly, prepared herself for Texas. Starting in the summer just preceding her arrival in Amarillo, she began to acquire a modernist sensibility—intuitive, comfortable with abstraction, experimental with color, and sensitive to alternate ways of composing. The new exposure came after a period of four years away from painting. In 1908, while at the Art Students League in New York, she had begun to question the exhausted academic realism still taught in art schools; those doubts and her family's strained finances spurred her to drop out and take a job as a commercial artist in Chicago. A bout of measles there left her eyes temporarily weakened, and she returned home to Virginia in 1910.

In the summer of 1912 O'Keeffe's two sisters persuaded her to join them in an art class taught by Alon Bement at the University of Virginia. The timing and the course content were just what she needed. Bement was an advocate of the design and educational principles of the eminent teacher Arthur Wesley Dow (1857–1922), whose ideas would rekindle O'Keeffe's desire to paint and stimulate her to think about teaching (fig. 3). Through four summers with Bement and her study directly with Dow at Columbia

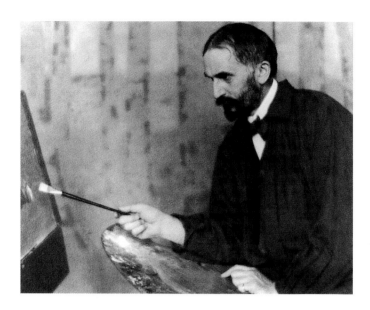

Figure 3
Alvin Langdon Coburn
Arthur Wesley Dow ca. 1902–13
Arthur Wesley Dow Collection and
Archives, Ipswich Historical Society,
Ipswich, Massachusetts

University's Teachers College in
New York (between 1914 and 1916),
O'Keeffe grafted the new ideas onto
her already well-developed technique.
"By this time," she recalled later, "I had
a technique for handling oil and water
color easily; Dow gave me something
to do with it."[12]

Something to do with it. A simple-
sounding gift, but expansive enough
to suggest Dow's profound and long-
standing influence on O'Keeffe. His
influence is one that has been widely

acknowledged, but not fully explored.
There are, in fact, several ways in
which Dow affected O'Keeffe's work,
and in turn her experience in Texas.
The first was in his classroom, when
she was his student.

Just before she ventured to Canyon
in 1916—in fact, as a prerequisite
for getting her teaching job there—
O'Keeffe enrolled for further study
with Dow at Columbia in order to
absorb more of his methods of teaching art. What did she learn from him?
Although he was a serious painter,
today Dow is best remembered as an
art educator, whose ideas were com-
municated to generations of American
students and teachers via his classic
text *Composition: A Series of Exercises in Art*

Structure for the Use of Students and Teachers,
first published in 1899. In it he out-
lined certain principles of composition
as ways to produce harmony in design.
Dow's introduction to the 1912 edi-
tion of the text contains his rationale
for the methods he developed. Long
before, argued Dow, art education
had gone awry; imitation had sadly
overwhelmed expressive intent. Soon
after Leonardo da Vinci's day, wrote
Dow, "Painting, which is essentially
a rhythmic harmony of colored
spaces, became sculptural, an imitation of modelling."[13] Painting, a
two-dimensional medium, should not
aspire to the three-dimensional do-
main of sculpture and architecture.
This was an idea shared by modernist
artists in Dow's day, and one destined
to become a core principle of modern-
ism for the next half-century.

Dow set about to restore art to its
proper role—one of expression, not
imitation. He proposed an approach
to art through structure, combining
certain elements and principles of
composition that could be applied to
"all work in drawing, painting, design-
ing and modelling—of house decora-
tion and industrial arts." So broad were
its applications, believed Dow, that a
person's life could reflect the rhythms
and harmonies achieved in their art.

This way of integrating art and life would hold tremendous appeal for Georgia O'Keeffe. And she would communicate it to her Texas students: "I liked to convey to them the idea that art is important in everyday life," she recalled. "I wanted them to learn the principle: that when you buy a pair of shoes or place a window in the front of a house or address a letter or comb your hair, consider it carefully, so that it looks well."[14]

Dow's compositional systems—what O'Keeffe would think of, summarily, as "filling space in a beautiful way"—were synthesized from both Western and Eastern aesthetics. As a student of Asian art, he investigated in considerable depth the great artistic and mythic traditions of the world. Dow's artistic ecumenism was fostered by his own mentor, Ernest Fenollosa (1853–1908), scholar of Chinese and Japanese art and Noh drama.

Fenollosa's lengthy residence in Japan and extensive European travel had prepared him to think in comparative terms of East and West. At the Museum of Fine Arts in Boston Fenollosa worked with a later-famous collection of Asian art he had helped assemble in Japan. In 1893 Fenollosa made Dow his assistant at the museum, passing along to him the elements of Chinese and Japanese aesthetics, such as *notan*, a method of light-and-dark patterning seen in the prints and paintings of Ukiyo-e masters.

In an effort to elevate "pure pictorial synthesis" above subject matter, Fenollosa, like others of his symbolist generation, likened poetry to painting, both of which he believed to contain the following vital elements:

Thought, sentiment, analogy, symbolism, the interpenetration of meaning, plane behind plane, sphere within sphere; the organic union of parts . . . even the spiritual significance of trees and rocks; and mountains, and water . . .[15]

Fenollosa's book *Epochs of Chinese and Japanese Art* sets forth many of the overarching principles of Asian aesthetics. Dow discussed Fenollosa's work in his classes, and included *Epochs* and Gonse's *L'art japonais* on the reading list for students during O'Keeffe's term at Columbia. In Fenollosa's book, and perhaps also in class discussions, O'Keeffe would have encountered the author's reverence for Sung landscape painters, whom Fenollosa regarded as supreme in their integration of landscape and symbol in the Chinese imagination. The Sung master's renderings of landscape, especially trees, mountains, and cliffs, often followed an artist-philosopher's pilgrimage into wilderness, where he meditated and sought to penetrate nature's inner harmonies. O'Keeffe would adopt this idea, whether from this source or another: that of solitude, of retreat into unpeopled spaces, to commune with nature and her innermost self.

With Fenollosa, Dow shared the ideas that form is relational and that nature provides the living example for such relations. These broad, poetic notions, with roots in Western and Eastern aesthetics, Dow distilled into a compositional system that could be taught to children and adults. In his book *Composition* he laid out a series of step-by-step exercises to analyze structure and to achieve harmony in design. It began with three elements: line, notan, and color. Those elements were the raw materials, which Dow then organized into five principles of composition:

1) Opposition: the simple meeting of two straight lines, as in doors and windows and in "landscape where vertical lines cut the horizon."

2) Transition: two straight lines with an added third—which may be modified into curves, as in architectural capitals or radiating forms.

3) Subordination: parts related to a single dominating element that determines the character of the whole. Axial structure, such as branches on a tree, petals on a stem, or architectural vaulting from a column are examples of this organization.

4) Repetition: the opposite of Subordination; rhythmic intervals of line or pattern. Dow notes that repetition is the basis of music and poetry, of harmonious border and allover surface patterns, but also of mundane forms such as railroads and fences.

5) Symmetry: equal balance of lines or shapes, as in windows on each side of a door.[16]

Georgia O'Keeffe never enslaved herself to Dow's principles of composition; she was much too independent and creative for that. And Dow himself urged individual interpretation. He wrote at the end of *Composition* of his goal: "The intention has been to reveal the sources of power; to show the student how to look within for the greatest help; to teach him not to depend on externals, not to lean too much on anything or anybody." It was perfectly in accord with O'Keeffe's own inclinations: to assert her own independence, to search out powerful motifs in nature, and to resist, when

necessary, critical opinion that would have stifled her creative risk-taking. Still, despite her growing independence, she would return to Dow's basic principles repeatedly over the next half-century, and we will see them affirmed in many canvases.

Thanks to Dow and Fenollosa, O'Keeffe would also remain a lifelong admirer of Asian art. In her classroom at Canyon she taught her students to use Japanese brush and ink. On the wall she placed many reproductions of decorative patterning from the Middle East and Asia, among which she included, as the sole example of "fine art," a Japanese print. Decades later, O'Keeffe was still surrounding herself with books on Asian art; her library at Abiquiu contained scores of texts, catalogues, and photographs at the time of her death. She remarked to an interviewer in 1974, "Of course my favorite is Chinese painting. I'd still say it's the best that's been done."[17]

Though she had completed her formal training with Dow when she moved to Canyon in 1916, O'Keeffe's connection with Dow did not end. In letters to friends, she referred to him as "Pa Dow," in the affectionate manner of many of his students. And, when her 1917 exhibition opened at Alfred Stieglitz's 291 gallery in New

York, she sent word of it to Dow. The eminent educator ventured downtown from Columbia to see his student's show, and wrote to her in Canyon that "I was interested in the simplicity of your designs and the harmonious rhythm that you had expressed so well." But he saw her wandering afield, and advised a return to more familiar territory: "It did seem to me, however, that there were too many of those vague things. I remember your excellent work in color printing and think it would be worth your while next time to show a greater variety."[18] Those "vague things" constituted O'Keeffe's bewildering (to Dow) shift toward abstraction—free and expansive like the Texas plains.

To Dow's qualified praise, O'Keeffe probably replied politely, holding her tongue in deference to her professor's prominence. When she wrote him later in the year, it was with thanks for his book *Theory and Practice of Teaching Art*, which she had apparently been using at Canyon. When he replied once more, Dow addressed her more as a colleague than as a student, lamenting the general indifference of Americans to the fine arts and asserting the importance of art education "to the lives and the work of those that come under its influence."[19]

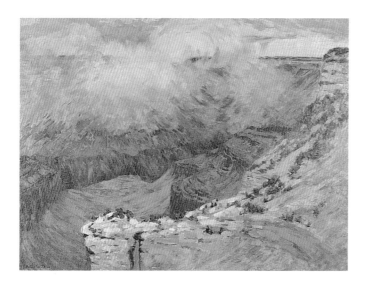

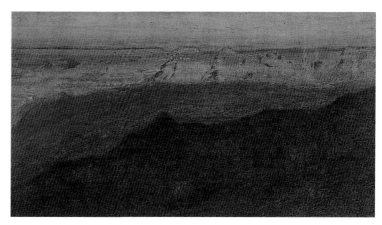

O'Keeffe, now a teacher and exhibiting painter, had taken her first steps on a journey away from Dow and from her own artistic past. But she was still grappling with ways to express the West Texas plains. In that struggle she thought again about Dow—this time not as a teacher, but as a painter who had also worked in the West. There Dow too had faced the difficulties of rendering profound meaning in nature. "It is not the province of the landscape painter," wrote Dow, "to represent so much topography, but to express an emotion; and this he must do by art."[20]

A few years before he encountered O'Keeffe, Dow had experienced an urge to paint "some of the *big things* of the world."[21] Partly in response to critics who saw his landscapes as decorative, Dow decided to undertake new subject matter—something so grand in scale that it would overwhelm familiar artistic concerns and demand to be dealt with on its own terms. He wanted to challenge usual concepts of scale and bring his own vision into direct collision with nature's vastness. He settled upon the Grand Canyon. In 1911 and 1912 Dow visited the Grand Canyon and painted it, using meticulous notes and photographs to assist him in capturing the fugitive effects of perspective disruptions, shifting color, flattened planes, and dramatically changing weather. From these efforts came such canvases as *Bright Angel Canyon* (1912; fig. 4) and *The Purple Shadow* (1912–13; fig. 5). For an exhibition of his Grand Canyon paintings at New

Figure 4 (*left*)
Arthur Wesley Dow
Bright Angel Canyon 1912
Oil on canvas
30 × 40¼ in. (76.2 × 102.2 cm)
Arthur Wesley Dow Collection and Archives, Ipswich Historical Society, Ipswich, Massachusetts

Figure 5 (*right*)
Arthur Wesley Dow
The Purple Shadow 1912–13
Oil on canvas
12 × 22 in. (30.5 × 55.9 cm)
Courtesy of the Tom Veilleux Gallery, Farmington, Maine

York's Montross Gallery in 1913, Dow wrote of the challenge he faced:

The Canyon is not like any other subject in color, lighting or scale of distances. It forces the artist to seek new ways of painting—its own ways. Its record of the world's beginning holds for us the romance of geology.[22]

During one of his Grand Canyon sojourns, Dow was joined by his friend, the prominent modernist photographer Alvin Langdon Coburn. Coburn (once close to Alfred Stieglitz and his circle) found the canyon equally challenging. His photographs explore unexpected light and shadow effects, as do Dow's own remarkable experiments in canyon photography.[23]

Dow's and Coburn's side-by-side experiences as painter and photographer were by no means unprecedented in the West; but Dow's paintings indicate clearly that the photographs gave him new access to the canyon's structure and optical distortions. Combined with his studies of the Canyon's extraordinary color shifts, photography at the Grand Canyon pushed Dow into new artistic territory. In *The Purple Shadow*, the rhythmic ranges of color and shadow approach abstraction in their simplification.

Dow was never a modernist, but his work at the Grand Canyon brought him as close as he would ever come to composing in mass and color, as he had already advocated in *Composition*. There too, he explored the concept of harmonious "visual music," to which Fenollosa had introduced him and with which many other advanced theorists (such as Wassily Kandinsky) were preoccupied in those years.

O'Keeffe knew Dow's paintings of the Grand Canyon, but she found them generally disappointing. Verbally, she dismissed them, with distinct condescension. In Canyon, not long after her arrival, she wrote to her friend Anita Pollitzer, "I can understand Pa Dow painting his pretty colored canyons—it must have been a great temptation—no wonder he fell."[24] But her dismissal of Dow's canyons is less certain in her work than in her words. While she may have rejected Dow's color—at times too pretty, too diffuse—his canyon paintings taught her much. She took lessons from them in addressing her own Texas canyons, particularly their formal structure. Even as she questioned and resisted Dow's landscapes, they reinforced for her one of his most vital precepts: that natural forms can be a vehicle for the artist's expression of emotion. O'Keeffe, intuitive by nature, followed Dow's anti-realist lead,

finding in nature the possibility for both formal invention and personal expression.

Moreover, Dow's Grand Canyon paintings, together with his own and Coburn's photography, suggest the ways the two arts could be mutually stimulating, a prototype for O'Keeffe's eventual engagement with Paul Strand, Alfred Stieglitz, and a handful of other influential photographers.

Dow's canyon paintings, particularly their color-banding and reductivist tendencies, would give O'Keeffe ideas about painting the Texas landscape. Most immediately, Dow pointed her toward new subjects available to her for the first time in Texas. In his Grand Canyon paintings lay implicit permission for her to marvel at and paint Palo Duro Canyon. And, because she objected to her former teacher's treatment of the Arizona canyon, she was challenged to address Palo Duro in more inventive ways.

East of the town of Canyon, the Palo Duro opens suddenly in the flatness of the plain. To O'Keeffe it looked like "slits in nothingness." Weather sometimes passed right over the canyon, without seeming to affect conditions below. Coronado's party had noted the phenomenon and, nearly four centuries later, O'Keeffe remarked on it in her letters.[25] Along with weather, time seemed to slide over Palo Duro Canyon, chiseled by water and wind some thousand feet below the plain. Being in the timeless expanse of the canyon reminded O'Keeffe to slow down, to savor the pairing of time measured in eons with that of the fast-changing light and weather. Working in what she called "a fever for painting and drawing," she marveled, ". . . this week has gone so fast that I want to grab it and make it stand still a minute—Time never went so fast befor—"[26]

Landforms

Palo Duro kept O'Keeffe enthralled for months. Soon after her arrival in Canyon she wrote Pollitzer of how it affected her:

Last night I couldn't sleep till after four in the morning—I had been out to the canyon all afternoon—till late at night—wonderful color—I wish I could tell you how big—and with the night the colors deeper and darker— cattle on the pastures in the bottom looked like little pin heads . . .[27]

As she lay awake during the night, the artist must have been reexperiencing the canyon in her mind. She and her sister Claudia, who was living with her that year, descended into its treacherous depths. "The only paths," recalled O'Keeffe, "were narrow, winding cow paths. There were sharp, high edges between long, soft earth banks so steep that you couldn't see the bottom." To keep from falling, the two sisters held opposite ends of a long stick, but the thrilling, dangerous descent stayed with her in dreams. "Those perilous climbs were frightening but it was wonderful to me and not like anything I had known before. . . .

Many drawings came from days like that, and later some oil paintings."[28]

Translated into the visual language of memory and dreams, the landscape of West Texas and Palo Duro provided a free range for O'Keeffe's imagination, perhaps nudging her along in her own inclinations toward abstraction. At many places the canyon stretched a mile wide. Within it grew junipers, wild plums, grapevines, and cottonwoods. The contrast of those growing things against the hot red of its sandstone formations provided the basis for many of O'Keeffe's paintings of the canyon.

The bold forms and coloration within the canyon allowed O'Keeffe to test her own skills in structural composition and in handling the watercolor medium. Works such as *Canyon Landscape* (1916–18; fig. 6) make reference to the redness of the canyon or its environs (this watercolor is part of *Georgia O'Keeffe: Canyon Suite,* a distinct exhibition).[29] O'Keeffe's sweeping arcs provide transition between verticals and horizontals, a reminder of Dow's principle of

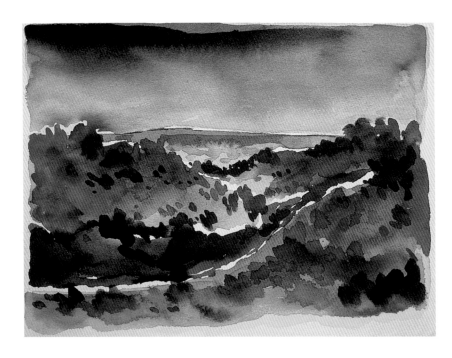

Figure 6
Georgia O'Keeffe
Canyon Landscape 1916–18
from the *Canyon Suite*
Watercolor on paper
9 × 12¼ in. (22.9 × 31.1 cm)
Collection of the Kemper Museum of
Contemporary Art & Design, Kansas
City, Missouri; Bebe and Crosby
Kemper Collection; Gift of the William
T. Kemper Charitable Trust, 1996.45

This watercolor is part of *Georgia O'Keeffe: Canyon Suite*, a distinct exhibition.

transition. Here O'Keeffe has combined two watercolor techniques: above, she washes a loose, watery sky; below her drier brush maintains a crisper precision. Air enters where narrow unpainted bands separate color areas, while the larger areas of deep green bring a balancing coolness to the red earth passages.

When O'Keeffe and Claudia left Texas for a summer vacation in Colorado in 1917, Georgia painted chromatically intense watercolors of overlapping hill and mountain forms, such as *Pink and Green Mountains No. 1* (cat. 5). Here the thin slivers of white between colored shapes return the eye

repeatedly to a consideration of surface flatness rather than depth.

Out of these Texas- and Colorado-born images O'Keeffe would later distill the power of the single, iconic mountain in landscape. Ultimately, and unforgettably, O'Keeffe would discover another flat-topped hill rising majestically in northern New Mexico and make many paintings of her beloved Pedernal.

As she was learning to do with many forms in Texas, O'Keeffe saw in nature shapes and movements she had already imagined, and in some cases already committed to paper. To understand the growing abstraction in her Texas landscapes, we must look back to the years immediately preceding her move to Canyon.

After her first period of study with Dow in the 1914–15 school term, and after three summers of work with his disciple Alon Bement, O'Keeffe took a teaching position for the 1915–16 school year in South Carolina. In her isolated months teaching there, O'Keeffe produced a series of remarkable large charcoal drawings, images that seem to express both the artist's own creative energies and the vitalist energies in nature. *Special No. 9* (1915; cat. 2) is one of these breakthrough compositions. O'Keeffe said years later that this image was "the drawing of a headache," adding, in her pragmatic way, "Well, I had the headache, why not do something with it?"[30]

She used the energy of the headache as the basis for something visual, and she came to terms with its sensory impact in *Special No. 9* by inventing a pictorial language for its throbbing effects. But this important drawing, while a prototype for many of her later images based on the immediacy of physical sensations, is not merely that. We see in its forms unmistakable allusions to nature: in the undulations of waves, the flicker of flames, the billowing of smoke or dust. And it is strongly reminiscent of compositions she had been studying in symbolist painting and Asian art; we see a similarly asymmetrical diagonal composition, together with waves, flamelike tendrils, and clouds recalling those in a famous Japanese *Scroll of Hells* from the twelfth century, part of which was reproduced in Fenollosa's book *Epochs of Chinese and Japanese Art.* O'Keeffe remarked that in the fall of 1915 she had "looked very carefully at Chinese and Japanese paintings and calligraphy . . ."[31]

Whatever its source, the free organic imagery in *Special No. 9* prepared O'Keeffe for nature's sweep, flow, and

powerful energies in West Texas. So did another of her large charcoals. *Drawing XIII* (1915; cat. 3) is a compressed, magnified, and recombined version of the forms in *Special No. 9.* In the latter drawing, vertical waves press against four bulbous shapes in the center, while a new element, a rising serrated line, frames them on the left. These lines and masses would not lie dormant long in O'Keeffe's memory bank. When she headed to Texas a few months later, she retrieved those forms and promptly reinserted them into landscape subjects. But it is clear that O'Keeffe thought of the 1915 charcoal abstractions, or at least a portion of them, as landscapes. Not long after she arrived in Canyon, she reminded Anita Pollitzer of them: "You possibly remember that my landscapes are always funny and these [new Texas ones] are not exceptions . . ."[32]

A Texas charcoal and subsequent oil clearly build on the formal elements O'Keeffe explored in *Special No. 9* and *Drawing XIII.* We see the charcoal *Special No. 15* (1916) in a portrait Alfred Stieglitz made of O'Keeffe in 1918 (fig. 7). The drawing and its companion painting, *Special No. 21* (1916; cat. 4) incorporating her experience of Palo Duro Canyon, show us how O'Keeffe's mind ranged back and forth

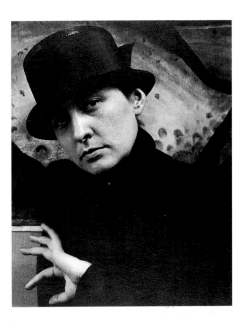

Figure 7
Alfred Stieglitz
Georgia O'Keeffe: A Portrait 1918
Palladium photograph
National Gallery of Art, Washington, D.C., Alfred Stieglitz Collection

from abstraction to realist-based imagery. Vestiges of Dow are clearly present in the oppositions of diagonals, curves, and straight lines. In O'Keeffe's oil version the landscape pulses with fiery color, like some primordial volcanic crucible starting to overflow. And the source of the heat erupts from within the hill, with no discernible light from a directional source. Here, the bulbous forms descended from her charcoal Specials

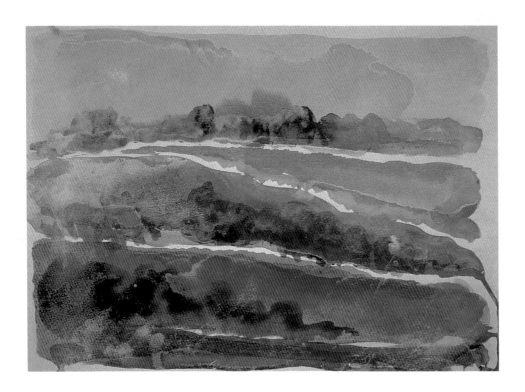

Figure 8
Georgia O'Keeffe
Across the Plains 1916–18
from the *Canyon Suite*
Watercolor on paper
10¼ × 14¾ in. (26 × 37.5 cm)
Collection of the Kemper Museum of
Contemporary Art & Design, Kansas City,
Missouri; Bebe and Crosby Kemper Collec-
tion; Gift of the Enid and Crosby Kemper
Foundation, 1996.48

This watercolor is part of *Georgia O'Keeffe:
Canyon Suite*, a distinct exhibition.

take on new identities as clouds and a
great tumbling flow of circular shapes
in the lower portion. Were those
shapes inspired by shrubs, or tumbling
water, or tiny cattle trailing along the
canyon bottom? We can't know for
certain; O'Keeffe's passages from
mind-forms to landscape forms flow in
both directions, teaching us to relax
such inquiries into an appreciation of
her inventiveness, not her literalness.
Of her own intense subjectivity, she
wrote to Anita Pollitzer, "I think all
the world has turned into what I'm
seeing."[33]

We see the way her mind traversed
the abstraction-realism continuum in
a group of works from a five-year period that begins in 1914 and extends
through her months at Canyon. The
earliest is her *Special No. 32* (cat. 1), a
pastel from 1914 containing similar
uncoiling energies and hot color, with
furling wavelike forms that demonstrate O'Keeffe's attention both to Art
Nouveau design and to the abstract inspiration she took from music. Next is
Red Landscape (cat. 6), a 1918 oil that
retains much of the brilliant redness of
O'Keeffe's *Special No. 21*. Violent up-
heaval is suggested in the surging red
forms that rise as hills on either side of
the sky/void. The form on the right in
Red Landscape points backward to *Special
No. 32* and ahead to several other oils
from 1918, notably O'Keeffe's Series 1
group. *Series 1, No. 1* (cat. 7), with its
lush, unfurling, organic shape, reverts
from landscape back into the abstract
mode she had explored four years earlier in *Special No. 32*. The massive cen-
tralized shape in *Series 1, No. 1* reasserts
O'Keeffe's desire to suggest, but not to
freeze, sensation as solid form. And
yet, in *Series 1, No. 1* her intersecting
arcs, hot color, and the triangle of
blue owe something unmistakable to
the landscape vision she had pursued
from her earliest months in Canyon,

particularly the Palo Duro–inspired painting *Special No. 21*. Finally, in considering this whole group of paintings we must think again of the probability of Asian influence. Hokusai's celebrated natural forms *The Wave* and *Fuji in Fine Weather from the South*, both composed in monumental rising curves, were reproduced together in Fenollosa's *Epochs of Chinese and Japanese Art*, that mother-lode text for O'Keeffe and all Dow's students.[34]

When her attention wandered from the majestic shapes inspired by the Texas canyons, O'Keeffe found a wealth of other landscape subjects nearby. She wrote to Alfred Stieglitz, "It seems so funny that a week ago it was the mountains I thought the most wonderful—and today its the plains—I guess it's the feeling of bigness in both that carries me away."[35]

The plains provided O'Keeffe with another kind of raw material for her continuing study of color in landscape. In the fall of 1916, her experiments were both stimulating and troubling to the newly arrived O'Keeffe. As in her canyon works, she was struggling to resist Dow's lead, but she had yet to establish a working color vocabulary of her own. Looking out at the autumn plains she saw a dazzling array of choices: "The plains

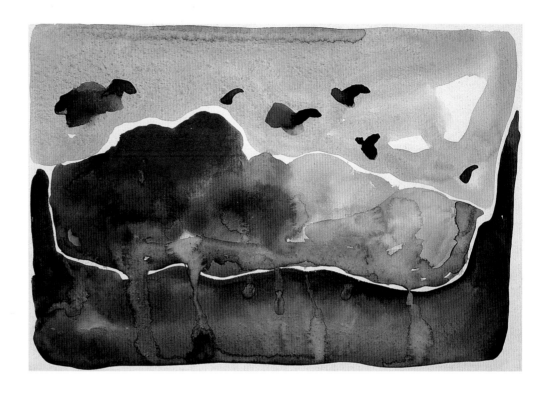

are very wonderful now—," she wrote Anita Pollitzer, "like green gold and yellow gold and red gold—in patches—and the distance blue and pink and lavender strips and spots—May sound like a Dow canyon—but its wonderful—specially in the evening—"[36]

She was not yet ready to eliminate any of that chromatic abundance from her paintings, so she made some watercolors rich with varieties of hue. *Autumn on the Plains* (*Georgia O'Keeffe Canyon Suite*, 1995 ed., plate 25) has all the colors she described to Pollitzer,

Figure 9
Georgia O'Keeffe
Landscape with Crows 1916–18
from the *Canyon Suite*
Watercolor on paper
7½ × 11 in. (19.1 × 27.9 cm)
Collection of the Kemper Museum of Contemporary Art & Design, Kansas City, Missouri; Bebe and Crosby Kemper Collection; Gift of Mr. and Mrs. R. Crosby Kemper, Jr., 1996.9

This watercolor is part of *Georgia O'Keeffe: Canyon Suite*, a distinct exhibition.

applied in patches, just as she saw them. Reducing her palette, O'Keeffe found ways to concentrate intensities and reorganize color into simpler shapes. In *Across the Plains* (1916–18; fig. 8), O'Keeffe replaces color patches with loose wedges of color, layered (again like in some of Dow's canyon paintings) one above the other (this watercolor is part of *Georgia O'Keeffe: Canyon Suite*, a distinct exhibition). This way of organizing landscape elements into dovetailed wedges would interest her in later years as well, as in *Storm Cloud, Lake George* (1923; cat. 9) and *Untitled (Bear Lake)* (1931; cat. 13).

Another way O'Keeffe reorganized the color patches she saw on her evening walks in Canyon was by containing them within sweeping curves. In her Texas watercolor *Landscape with Crows* (1916–18; fig. 9), a deep violet band frames and holds the red, orange, and gold elements beyond (this watercolor is part of *Georgia O'Keeffe: Canyon Suite*, a distinct exhibition). A few years later nature would again provide such a curving form to contain color: in *Lake George with Crows* (1921; cat. 8) the waterline is a curving, embracing shape. Here O'Keeffe deliberately plays with modernist flatness and spatial depth, creating formal tensions in

an apparently tranquil painting. First she floats three crows over the seemingly distant expanse of water. Simultaneously, at the far right, she denies that depth when the lake's edge stubbornly presses forward as a curved white slice, very much on the painting's surface.

A few years later, in *Lake George* (1924; cat. 10), O'Keeffe makes the waterline function quite differently as a formal element. Instead of being viewed from high above, it stretches flat across at the viewer's eye level, then rises at the far left as a narrow blue ribbon, rhyming gently with three wavelike forms on the lake's surface. The reductivist silhouette of dark hills above contrasts in solidity with the evanescent forms below. *Lake George* is a study in loose axial symmetry, with a form almost like a horizontal feather.

Continuing to reduce and refine the visual embrace of land and water, O'Keeffe painted *Wave, Night* in 1928 (cat. 11). In her 1976 book, she recalled her 1920s ocean experience of "watching the waves come in, spreading over the hard wet beach—the lighthouse steadily bright far over the waves in the evening when it was almost dark."[37] Both the artist's words and her painting are understated,

distilled recollections of that unforgettable experience in nature.

Taking what she first learned in Texas about simplifying and consolidating shapes in landscape, O'Keeffe continued to apply those formal strategies to landscapes in other places. Visiting New Mexico in 1930, O'Keeffe encountered another dark range of hills, something like those in her Lake George backgrounds. Now, instead of a watery foreground, she returned to the dry, chromatically intense earth she had encountered in Texas. In *Dark Mesa and Pink Sky* (1930; cat. 12) the atmosphere and cool tonalities of Lake George are replaced by the sharp, assertive outlines of bare hills and crystalline air. Of these paintings, made near Alcalde, New Mexico, O'Keeffe would later recall,

It was the shapes of the hills there that fascinated me. The reddish sand hills with the dark mesas behind them. It seemed as though no matter how far you walked you could never get into those dark hills, although I walked great distances.[38]

Reductivist, spare yet sensuous, *Dark Mesa and Pink Sky* reconfigures the black and red of O'Keeffe's fiery Palo Duro paintings. Above an impenetrable mass of background hills she paints a fragile pink sky of the kind destined to disappear in minutes. Below, the organic sand hills—all undulating curves—frame the blackness, while a pair of red arcs rise on the right, like quotation marks from some primordial geological text. At the left, balancing them, a long slow curve (changing from red to brown) sweeps the eye from the middle of the left edge downward to the center of the painting's lower edge. It is a classic example of Dow's principle of transition: a curve bridging horizontal and vertical lines. The painting's edges provide the only straight lines in *Dark Mesa and Pink Sky*, the only relief from the incessant heaving movement in the red and brown hills. Lacking a single shrub or blade of grass, the place is dead, yet pulsing with life, like O'Keeffe's hot-earth paintings from Texas. *Dark Mesa and Pink Sky* is one of O'Keeffe's private, unknowable places. The opacity and iconic spareness of these mysterious sites invest them with power, like a liturgy spoken in a hieratic tongue. In the canny intensity of her pictorial combinations, O'Keeffe has made of *Dark Mesa and Pink Sky* what Dow liked to call a "power source" in nature.

Powerful too are the dark, muscular shapes of *Grey Hills* (1942; cat. 14), painted from an isolated place in northwest New Mexico about 150 miles from O'Keeffe's home at Ghost Ranch. She called it the Black Place, and traveled there repeatedly in the 1930s and '40s, camping along its windy edges and painting its wrinkled surfaces and eery banded coloration.

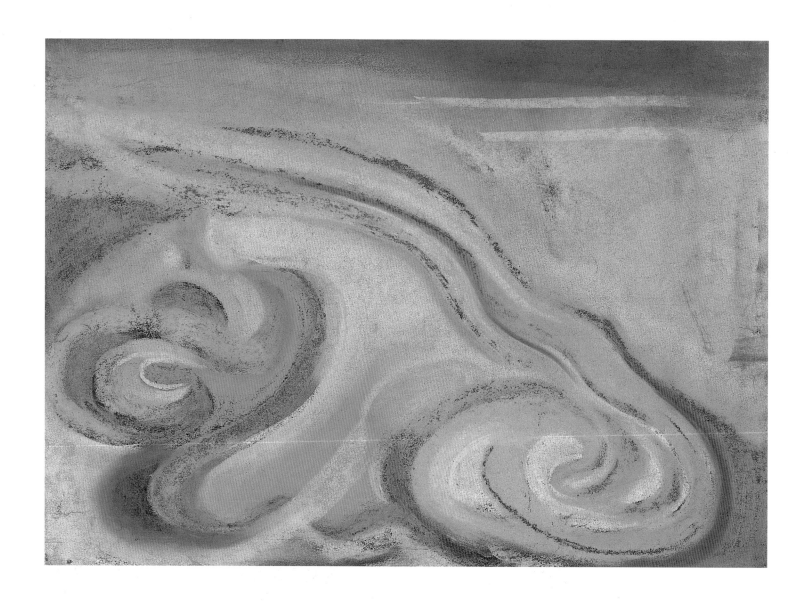

Landforms/1
Special No. 32
1914
Pastel on paper
National Museum of American Art,
Smithsonian Institution

Landforms/2
Special No. 9
1915
Charcoal on paper
The Menil Collection

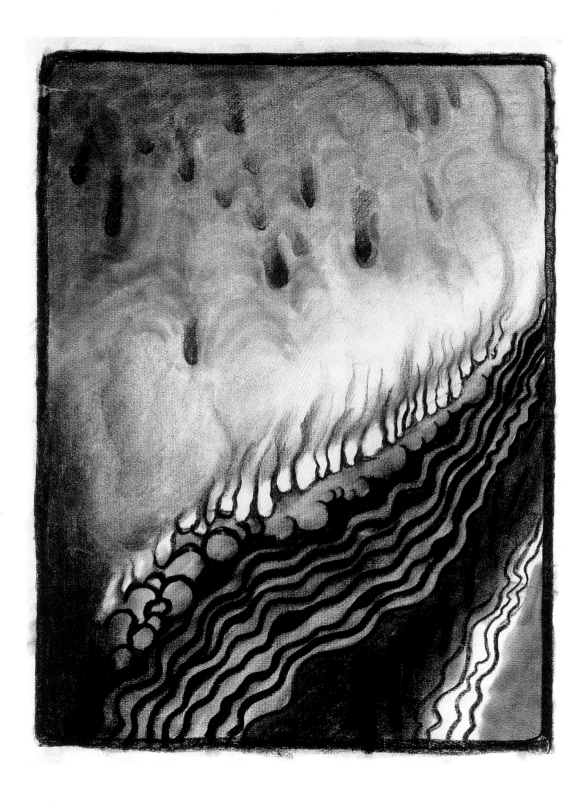

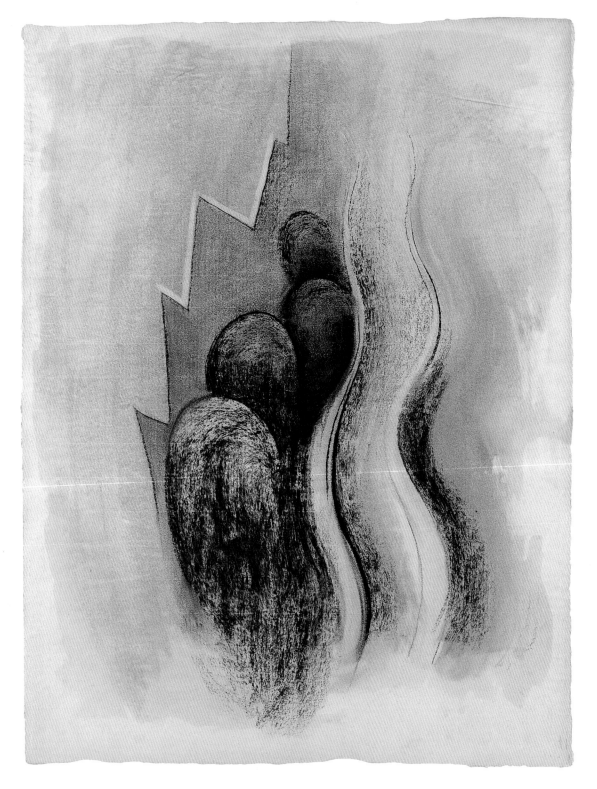

Landforms/3
Drawing XIII
1915
Charcoal on paper
The Metropolitan Museum
of Art

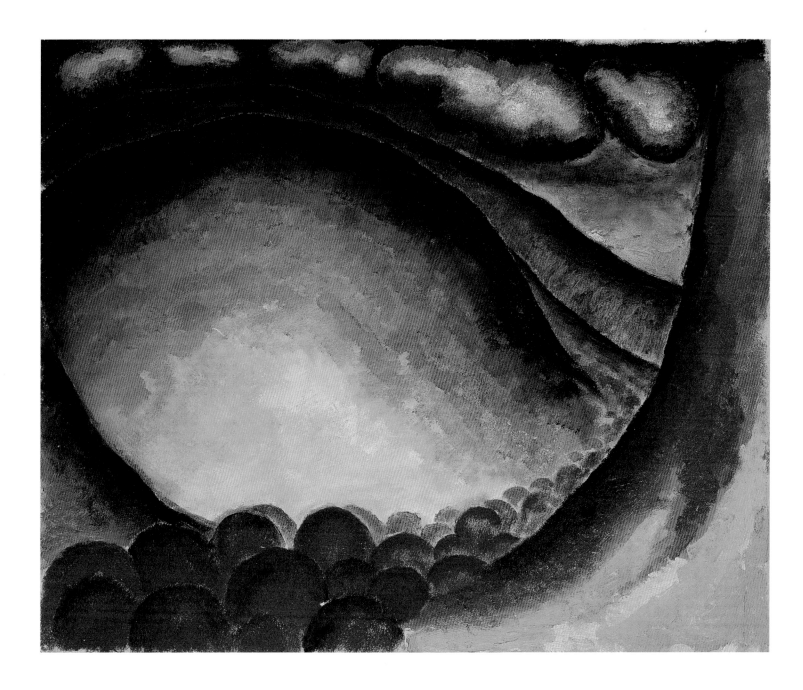

Landforms/4
Special No. 21 (Palo Duro Canyon)
1916
Oil on canvas
Museum of Fine Arts, Museum of New Mexico

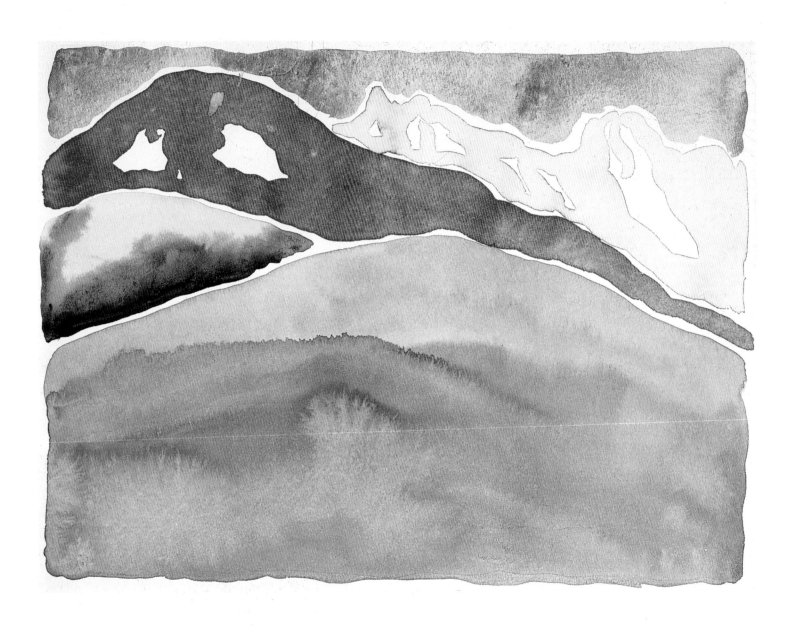

Landforms / 5
Pink and Green Mountains No. 1
1917
Watercolor on paper
Spencer Museum of Art, The University
of Kansas

Landforms/6
Red Landscape
1918
Oil on board
Panhandle-Plains Historical Museum

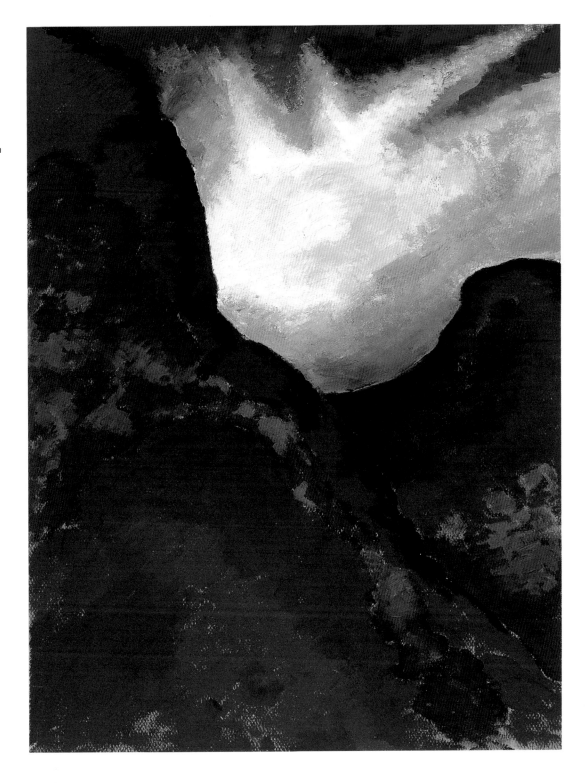

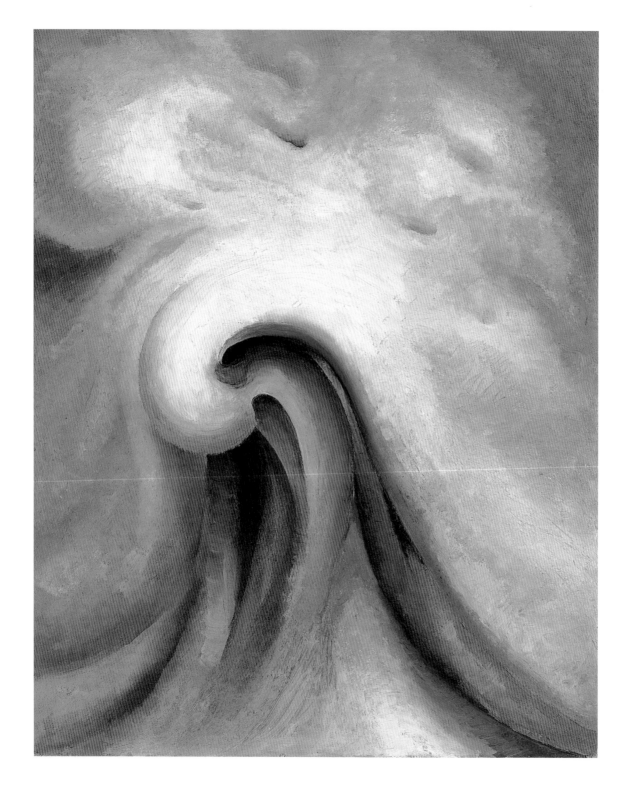

Landforms/7
Series 1, No. 1
1918
Oil on board
Amon Carter Museum

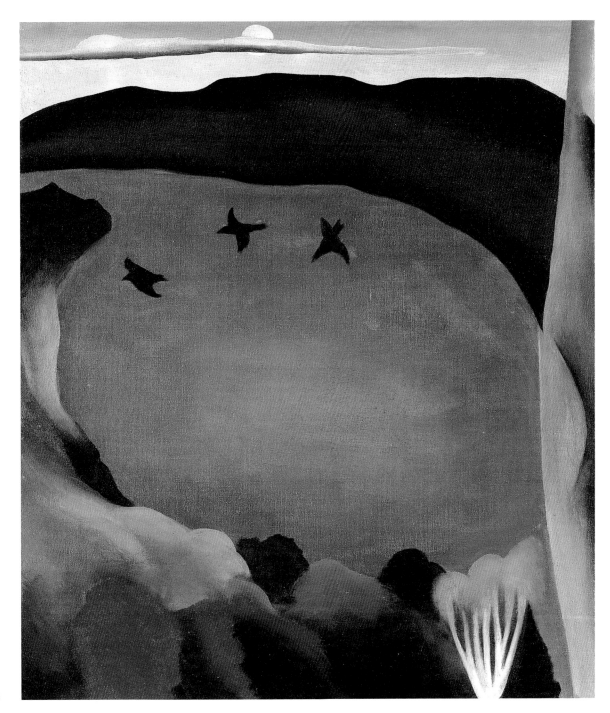

Landforms/8
Lake George with Crows
1921
Oil on canvas
National Gallery of Canada

"I think all the world
has turned into
what I'm seeing."

Landforms/9
Storm Cloud, Lake George
1923
Oil on canvas
Private Collection

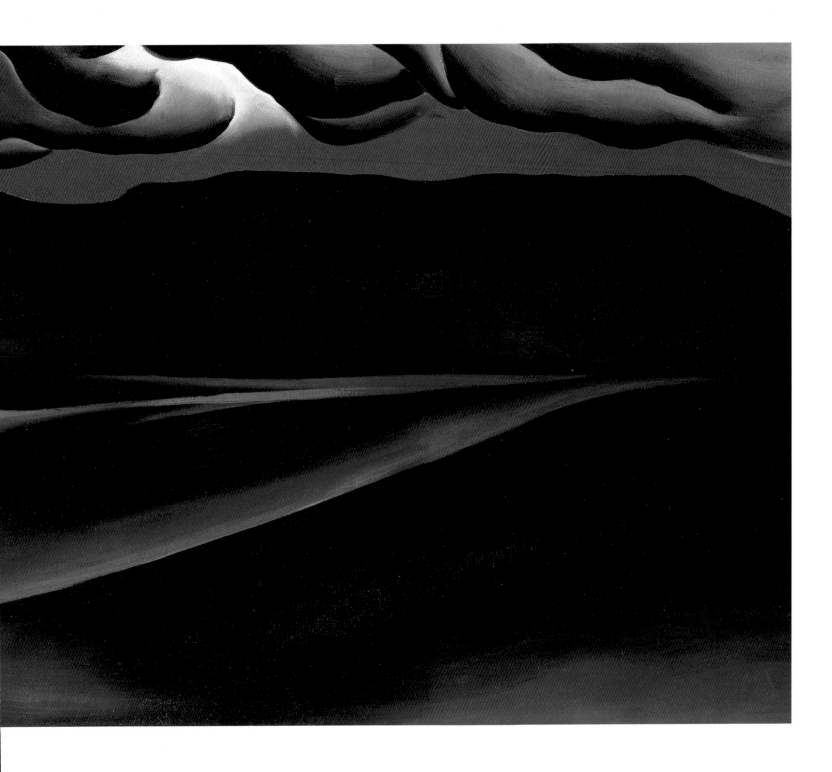

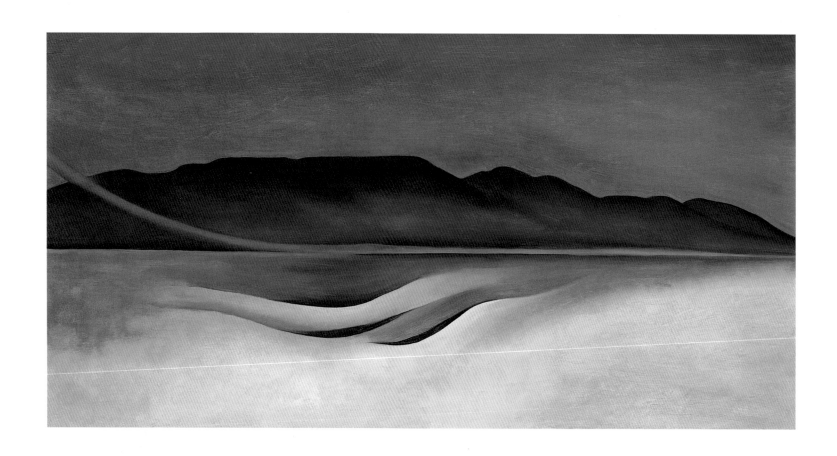

Landforms/10
Lake George
1924
Oil on canvas
Barbara and James Palmer

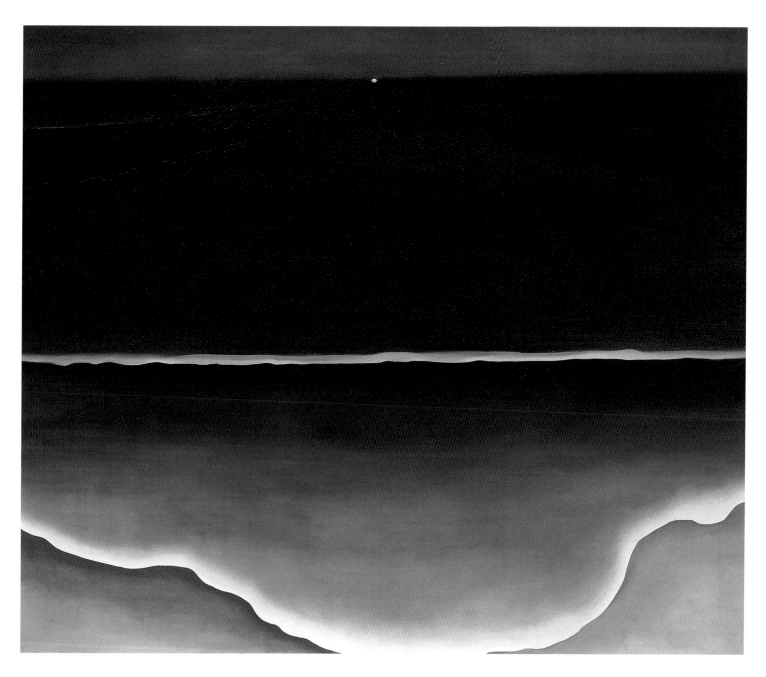

Landforms/11
Wave, Night
1928
Oil on canvas
Addison Gallery of American Art, Phillips Academy

Landforms/12
Dark Mesa and Pink Sky
1930
Oil on canvas
Amon Carter Museum

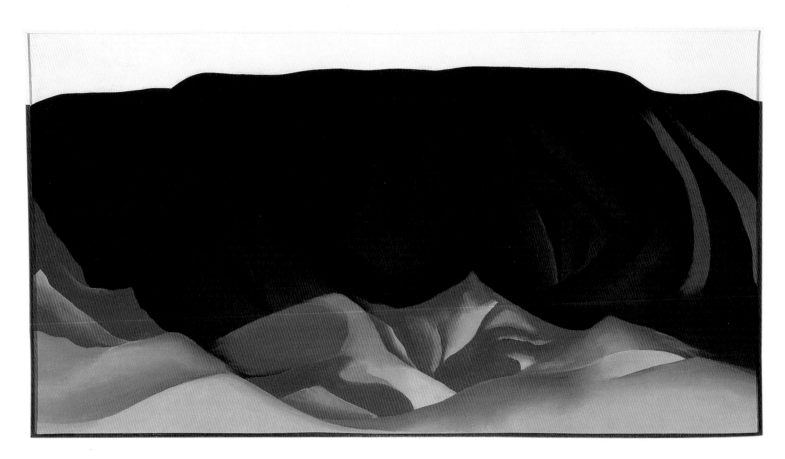

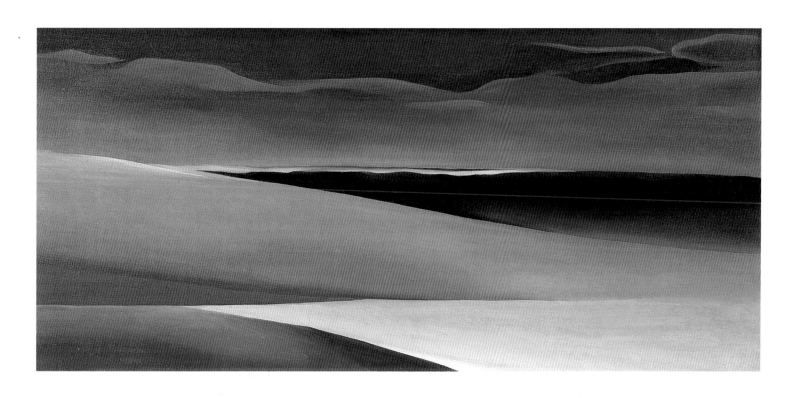

Landforms/13
Untitled (Bear Lake)
1931
Oil on canvas
Museum of Fine Arts, Museum of New Mexico

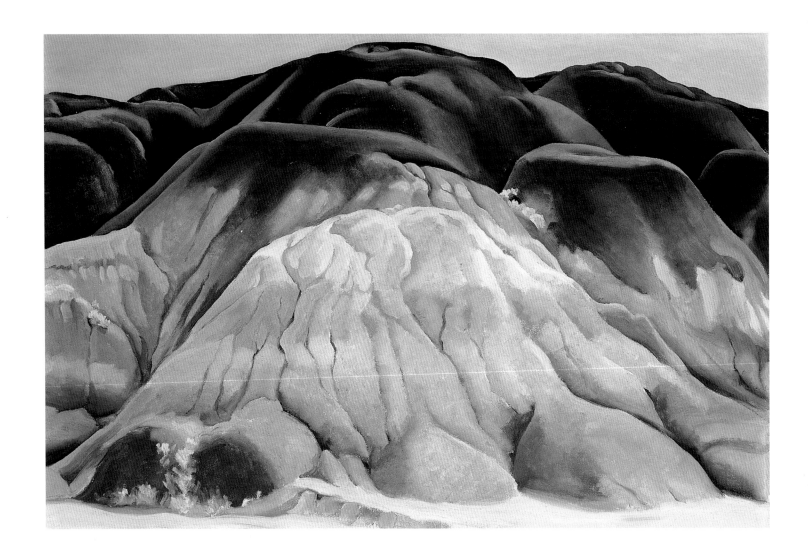

Landforms/14
Grey Hills
1942
Oil on canvas
Indianapolis Museum of Art

Light and the origin of meaning

Three months before she moved to Canyon, while teaching a final summer session at the University of Virginia, O'Keeffe had begun to think about light in a new way. From Charlottesville she wrote to her friend Anita Pollitzer:

I had to go up to the University after dark—and saw for the first time a new light arrangement that makes the rotunda and the people walking around it very wonderful—It was so surprising—Light is thrown at it—from the bushes or somewhere—I didn't notice how it happened. I only noticed that it gave all sorts of fine effects from different views—I think I'm going to make something from it—hope I am—[39]

Sooner than she might have expected, O'Keeffe did make "something from it." What she saw that night in Virginia, the "fine effects" produced by light, became part of O'Keeffe's store of visual memories, to be withdrawn and used in Texas. There, in the Panhandle, the dry air produced extraordinary light, particularly at dawn and dusk. As she walked into the sunset during her early weeks at Canyon, she was astounded by the elements at play in the sky. To Anita she wrote: "Tonight I walked into the sunset—to mail some letters—The whole sky—and there is so much of it out here—was just blazing—and grey-blue clouds were rioting all through the hotness of it—"[40]

An extraordinary group of sunset paintings resulted from O'Keeffe's experience of crepuscular sky effects. When dust hovered above the horizon, the colors intensified. In some of her early Texas watercolors of sunsets, the waning light burns almost like a flame, muffled by the lowering dark. On other evenings the light refused to give up without a fight: explosions of violent color, as in *Red, Blue and Green* (1915; cat. 15), enfold tremendous energies, while *Abstraction Pale Sun* (1917; cat. 16) renders a more delicate visual impression.

From the spectacular late-day effects of sunsets, O'Keeffe followed light's passage from day into glittering night, complex and radiant. Here, O'Keeffe is rediscovering the potency of the single image, the power of the center.

In the way Ernest Fenollosa had described, O'Keeffe was inventing, step by step, a language of artistic relationships, moving from the center outward. Fenollosa had described such visual communication as "a pregnant language; rich, juicy, significant, full words, charged with intense meaning at the center, like a nucleus, and then radiating out toward infinity, like a great nebula."[41]

O'Keeffe's monumental Evening Star series celebrates that radiant power of light in the evening sky. She recalled, years later, that as she walked out onto the Texas plains, "The evening star would be high in the sunset sky when it was still broad daylight. That evening star fascinated me. . . . I had nothing but to walk into nowhere and the wide sunset space with the star."[42]

In a stunning series of Canyon watercolors O'Keeffe celebrated the vibrant energy radiating from that star. *Evening Star, No. V* (1917; cat. 17) is a magnificent zenith of that group, at once loose and controlled. Light becomes more liquid in *Evening Star VII* (1917; fig. 10), softer and less distinct.

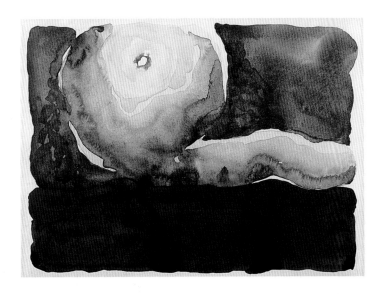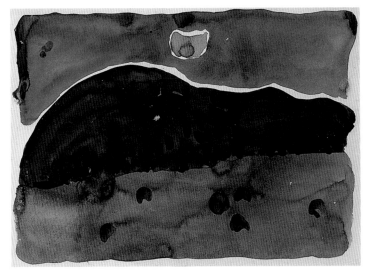

Figure 10 (*left*)
Georgia O'Keeffe
Evening Star VII 1917
Watercolor on paper
8⅞ × 11⅞ in. (22.5 × 30.2 cm)
Collection of the Georgia O'Keeffe
Museum, Santa Fe, Gift of the Burnett
Foundation

Figure 11 (*right*)
Georgia O'Keeffe
Evening 1916
Watercolor on paper
8⅞ × 12 in. (22.5 × 30.5 cm)
Collection of the Georgia O'Keeffe
Museum, Santa Fe, Gift of the Burnett
Foundation and The Georgia O'Keeffe
Foundation

Embraced by concentric rings, these assertive images have their source in nature but connect metaphorically with larger ideas about creativity current in O'Keeffe's day. In the year O'Keeffe went to Canyon, Ezra Pound expounded on his vorticist notion of artistic "seeing," writing:

The image is not an idea. It is a radiant node or cluster, it is what I can, and must perforce, call a VORTEX, from which, and through which, and into which ideas are constantly rushing.[43]

Whether or not she knew of the imagery formulated by Fenollosa and Pound, the motif of radiating light persisted in O'Keeffe's Texas paintings of the night sky. We cannot know for certain in some of them what the source of that light is—setting sun, star, or moon. *Evening* (1916; fig. 11) casts one of those luminous orbs above the advancing dark. We know from her letters that O'Keeffe looked carefully at all the events in the evening sky above West Texas. Walking out from Canyon, she recalled the stunning impression of a plains moonrise:

Then the moon rose right up out of the ground after we got out on the plains again—battered a little where he bumped his head—but enormous—There was no wind—it was just big and still . . . A great place to see the nighttime because there is nothing else.[44]

Sunrises were as captivating as the evening's light effects. An early morning bus ride from Amarillo to Canyon chased a spectacular sunrise, and

O'Keeffe returned home awestruck, determined to paint its effects. Years later, she tried to describe what she was after in her sunrise paintings from Texas. "The light would begin to appear," she remembered, "and then it would disappear and there would be a kind of halo effect, and then it would appear again. The light would come and go for quite a while before it finally came."[45] Those comings and goings of fickle dawns pressed her to record their halating effects. If morning light could be given a shape, O'Keeffe determined to find it. In *First Light Coming on the Plains* (1916–18; fig. 12), O'Keeffe paints with a rough urgency, as though fighting to fix the fugitive sensation (this watercolor is part of *Georgia O'Keeffe: Canyon Suite*, a distinct exhibition). By contrast, *Light Coming on the Plains I* (1917; fig. 13) pulses gently with subtle gradations of light. These and several other studies of Panhandle mornings suggest the birth of light in various stages of the dawn. In such moments, as Norman O. Brown writes, "Meaning is in the play, or interplay, of light."[46]

O'Keeffe visualized that interplay of light in many subsequent subjects. Nearly ten years after her last departure from Texas she revisited the expanding rings of sunlight behind fiery

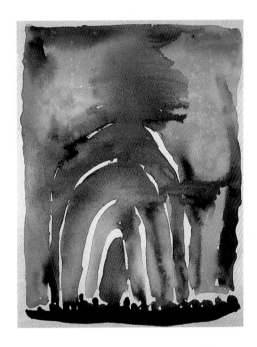

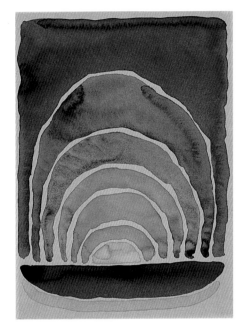

Figure 12
Georgia O'Keeffe
First Light Coming on the Plains 1916–18
from the *Canyon Suite*
Watercolor on paper
12½ × 9½ in. (31.8 × 24.1 cm)
Collection of the Kemper Museum of Contemporary Art & Design, Kansas City, Missouri; Bebe and Crosby Kemper Collection; Gift of the Enid and Crosby Kemper Foundation, 1996.36

This watercolor is part of *Georgia O'Keeffe: Canyon Suite*, a distinct exhibition.

Figure 13
Georgia O'Keeffe
Light Coming on the Plains I 1917
Watercolor on paper
11⅞ × 8⅞ in. (30.2 × 22.5 cm)
Collection of the Amon Carter Museum, Fort Worth

hills, in *Red Hills, Lake George* (1927; cat. 18). Both for its study of light and for the striking redness and spare shapes in the landscape, this painting harks back to the dry hillocks of her Palo Duro paintings. And it forecasts O'Keeffe's fascination with the red hills of New Mexico, which she would begin to paint only two years later.

In the 1920s O'Keeffe studied the interplay of light within flowers. Her remarkable series of jacks-in-the-pulpit from the spring of 1930 hybridizes the effects of halating light—begun in 1916 with her vision of the university rotunda in Charlottesville—with several concerns, including the bulbous forms in her *Drawing XIII* and their progeny born in the Texas paintings. By the time she reached a culminating point in *Jack-in-the-Pulpit VI* (1930; cat. 20), O'Keeffe had reduced the flower to its innermost essence. With its surrounding aura of light, this sixth jack brought the subject from representational beginnings (the first three in the series) back through a reductivist loop to this final, spare form wrapped in light. O'Keeffe once again had captured the power of the single iconic image, borrowed from nature but reinvented as something akin to autobiography. The presence and absence of light was always a vital

element in O'Keeffe's consciousness, but never more clearly so than in her *Black Abstraction* (1927; cat. 19). Painted in response to losing consciousness under surgical anesthesia, it is a painting from the threshold between waking and sleep. Determined to remain conscious as long as possible, O'Keeffe watched a skylight in the operating room shrink to a white dot, which she recorded a few weeks later as the glowing center of dark concentric circles, in shape reminiscent of her Evening Star series. *Black Abstraction* uses halating light as a symbol for artistic consciousness, in a manner akin to the way O'Keeffe's literary contemporary Virginia Woolf connected life and light. "Life," wrote Woolf, "is a luminous halo, a semi-transparent envelope surrounding us from the beginning of consciousness to the end."[47]

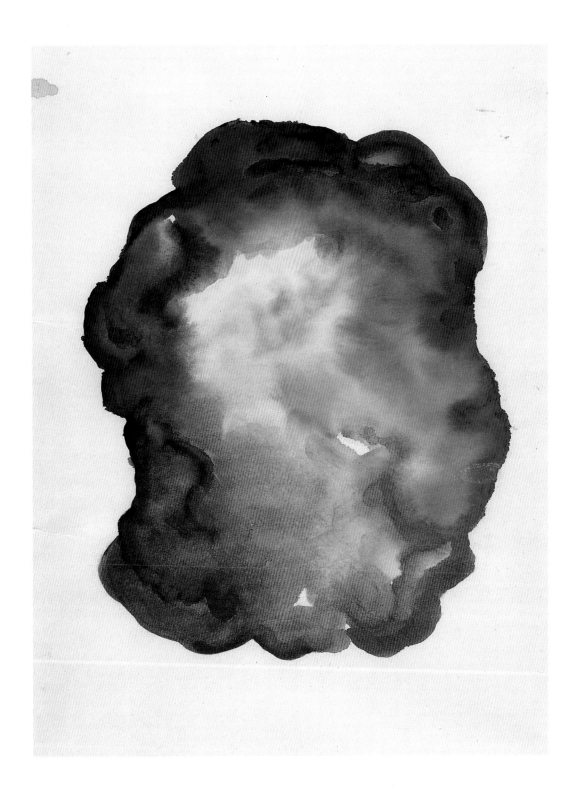

Light/15
Red, Blue and Green
1915
Watercolor on paper
Tobin Foundation

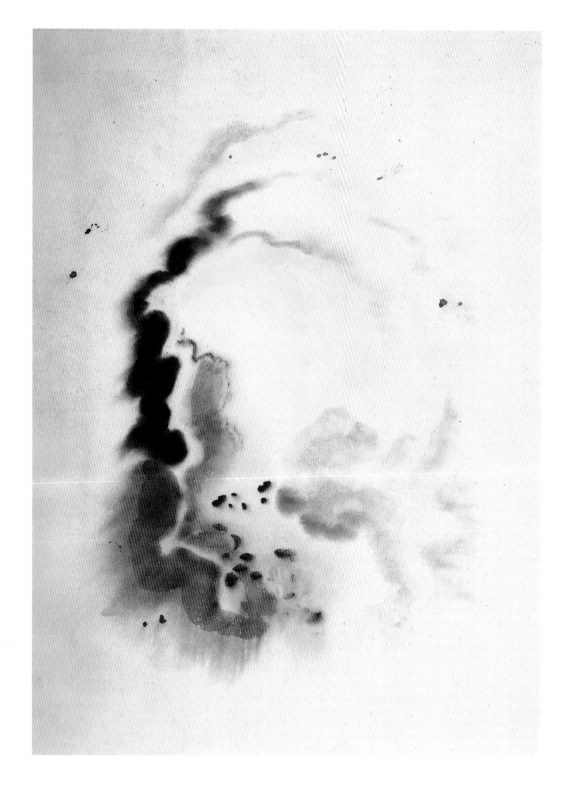

Light/16
Abstraction Pale Sun
1917
Watercolor
The Gerald Peters Gallery

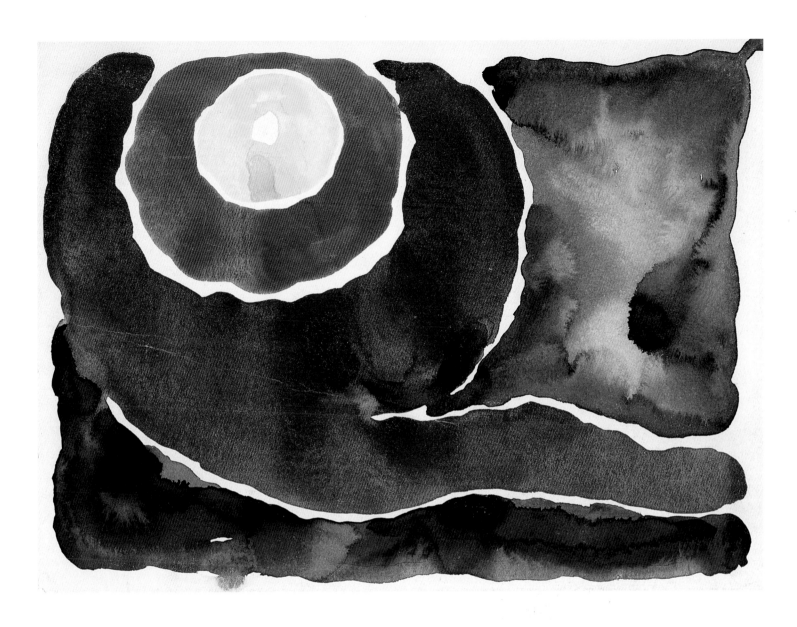

Light/17
Evening Star, No. V
1917
Watercolor
The McNay Art Museum

"I had nothing but to walk
into nowhere and the wide
sunset space with the star."

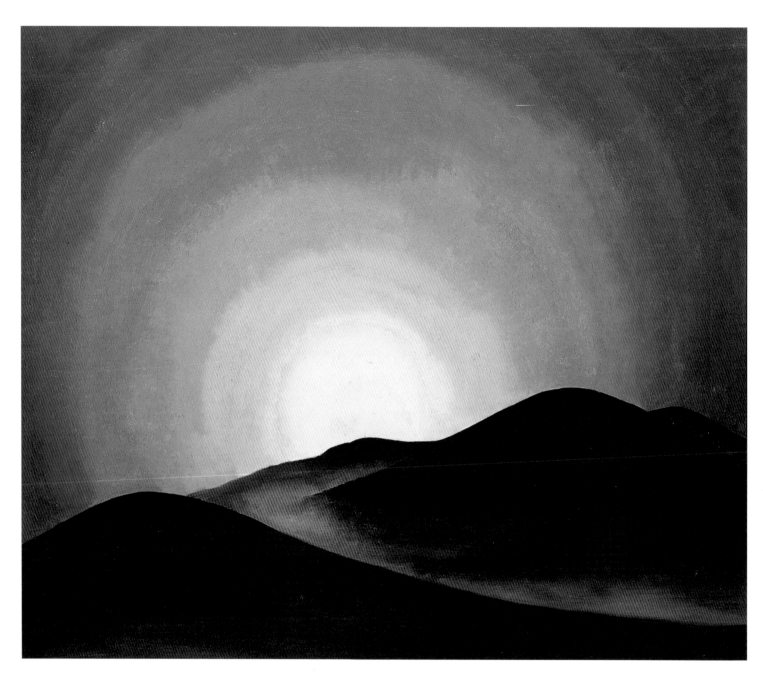

Light/18
Red Hills, Lake George
1927
Oil on canvas
The Phillips Collection

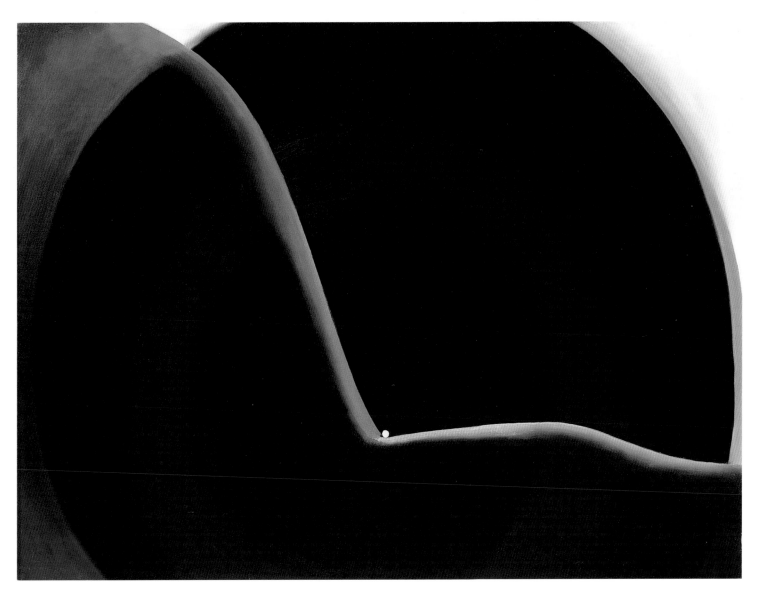

Light/19
Black Abstraction
1927
Oil on canvas
The Metropolitan Museum of Art

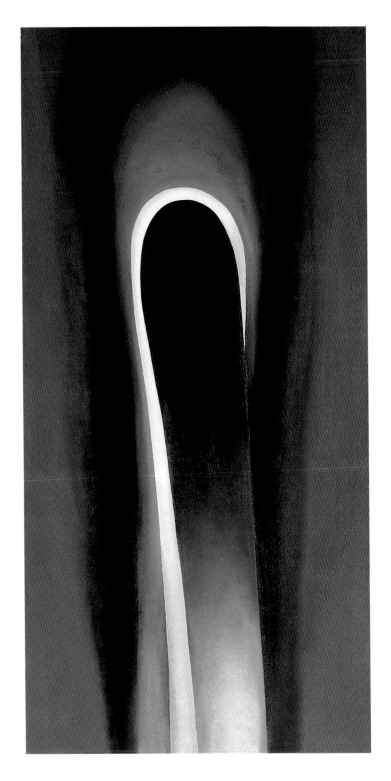

Light/20
Jack-in-the-Pulpit VI
1930
Oil on canvas
National Gallery of Art

Making Order: Geometric patterns

The vastness of the great duality of West Texas—sky and open land, both without visible limits—inspired O'Keeffe to stretch her own conceptions of space. This she did with increasing comfort, obeying her own inclinations to abstract and to use the power of light as unifying image. But Dow had reminded her that he (and perhaps others) saw "too many of those vague things" in her 1917 New York show. Whether she still cared for Dow's opinion when she had earned unstinting praise from Stieglitz is debatable. Still, she was using Dow's methods in her teaching, including his exercises in spatial organization. Perhaps those, combined with her own proclivity for order, encouraged her to introduce some geometric patterning in her Texas watercolors.

Maybe it began in Amarillo, where many houses around the turn of the century were painted a cheerful *amarillo*—yellow. And perhaps it was one of those that O'Keeffe remembered as *Yellow House* (1917; cat. 21). As a high school teacher in that town she looked for projects her students could work with from their own visual experience. The town's forthright frame houses were one point of beginning. Seen frontally, their plain perimeters acted as frames into which elements like doors and windows had been inserted by the builders. Usually they were symmetrical, typically with a pair of windows flanking a central door. O'Keeffe's sturdy *Yellow House* may be a reminder of her teaching experience, and it may refer as well to the interest both Dow and Stieglitz had in the art of children.[48] The naiveté of children's art, which seemed fresh and original to many artists during that decade, seemed to offer a model of continual renewal for the painter, a prospect of repeated self-birth. As Constantin Brancusi would say it, "When we are no longer children, we are already dead."

Besides its reminiscence of children's art, *Yellow House* also served to illustrate—for O'Keeffe, and possibly for her students—at least two of the principles she had learned from Arthur Dow. In *Composition,* from which O'Keeffe derived exercises for her students, Dow began with examples from the art of the past, then directed students to "find examples in nature and draw [them]."[49] In his book, Dow illustrated opposition in the refined proportions of a Greek post-and-lintel doorway. Other equally suitable examples of opposition existed closer to home; in every rectangle, in plaid design, and "in landscape where vertical lines cut the horizon." West Texas students, whose visual world held an abundance of horizon, would have no trouble finding abrupt intersections of the vertical and horizontal. Every house, every telegraph pole, every tree embodied Dow's oppositional principle.

But even more striking in O'Keeffe's *Yellow House* is the element of symmetry, which Dow described as "the most common and obvious way of satisfying the desire for order." The exact balance of "windows each side of a door" was an easily seen example, he suggested. By painting in the manner of a child, often symmetrical in the extreme, O'Keeffe illustrated the unrelieved severity of symmetry. She

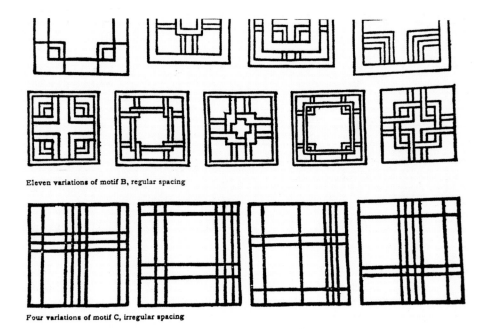

Eleven variations of motif B, regular spacing

Four variations of motif C, irregular spacing

Figure 14
Arthur Wesley Dow
Linear compositions in squares from
*Composition: A Series of Exercises in Art
Structure for the Use of Students and Teachers*
(New York: Doubleday, 1938), p. 32

employed straight lines almost exclusively, as Dow advised the beginner, allowing for the "slight waverings" he said enhanced the character of straight lines.

Embodying repose and a sense of completeness in design, *Yellow House* points to the compositional possibilities of symmetry, as well as to its limitations. It also demonstrates what can be done with groups of rectangles arranged within a larger rectangle, one of the many exercises Dow assigned to his readers (fig. 14) and one repeated by O'Keeffe with her own students in Texas. Years later she recalled, "I'd get them to draw a square and put a door

in it somewhere—anything to start them thinking about how to divide a space."[50] What *Yellow House* showed O'Keeffe's students (and no doubt reinforced in her own mind) was that opposition, symmetry, and repetition could produce one kind of design harmony—a kind of static subdivision of flattened space. In her early weeks at Canyon, when O'Keeffe asked her friend Anita Pollitzer to send reproductions of fine classical design—Greek pottery, textiles, and Persian plates—she was gathering for her students historical examples of this kind of surface patterning.

At other times in Texas O'Keeffe used architectural elements as the basis for alternate compositional schemes. In *Roof with Snow* and its accompanying studies (1917; cats. 22, 23, and 24), O'Keeffe floated loosely rendered patches of snow on a roof, softening the rigid placement of windows and chimneys.

Though she would ultimately come to prefer the tensional dynamism of more sophisticated compositional schemes, O'Keeffe would return periodically throughout her career to the architectural severity of houses, doors, and windows to work out certain formal questions. Lingering was the influence of Dow's exercises with squares

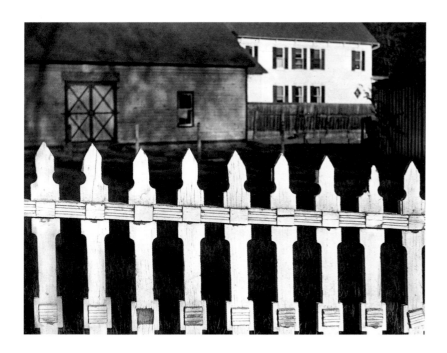

Figure 15
Paul Strand
The White Fence, Port Kent, New York 1916
Silver gelatin print
10 × 13 in. (25.4 × 33 cm)

looking at things and seeing them as I thought you might photograph them—Isn't that funny—making Strand photographs for myself in my head . . ."[51]

O'Keeffe did not have to rely solely on her memory of Strand's images, for he soon sent her prints. It was a period when Strand was merging the formal concerns of abstraction with the factual accuracy of the camera, and the results were revolutionary. O'Keeffe mentioned receiving several Strand prints in July: "Why you know I love it all[.] The prints you sent me—the bowls—the shadows."[52] The "bowls" were almost certainly Strand's famous photograph *Abstraction, Bowls* (1914 or 1915), an orchestration of intersecting circular forms. The "shadows" must refer to his celebrated *Abstraction, Porch Shadows* (1914 or 1915). Unnamed by O'Keeffe, but probably among the many other prints he sent her that summer, was his equally famous *White Fence, Port Kent, New York* (1916; fig. 15). Of this photograph, Strand said that it was an application of the lessons he learned in photographing the bowls and porch shadows. Treating the foreground fence as a flat, geometric element, behind which he situated the starkly geometric forms of a barn and house, Strand thought of this

and rectangles. Building on that, O'Keeffe would experiment with modules of geometric form, often within the form of a grid. In 1917 that inclination was underscored powerfully by O'Keeffe's contact with Paul Strand.

When she went East late in May of that year, she met Paul Strand, a rising star among the Stieglitz circle. Immediately they felt a kinship and began corresponding. She first wrote him, in fact, on the train trip back to Texas on June 3. O'Keeffe liked both the man and the work, and she told him so forthrightly: "And Ive been wanting to tell you again and again how much I liked your work—I believe Ive been

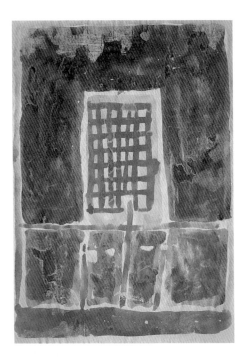

Figure 16
Georgia O'Keeffe
Red House with Fence and Door 1916–18
from the *Canyon Suite*
Watercolor on paper
10½ × 7½ in. (26.7 × 19.1 cm)
Collection of the Kemper Museum of
Contemporary Art & Design, Kansas
City, Missouri; Gift of Mr. and Mrs.
Gerald Peters, Santa Fe, 1996.56

This watercolor is part of *Georgia O'Keeffe:
Canyon Suite,* a distinct exhibition.

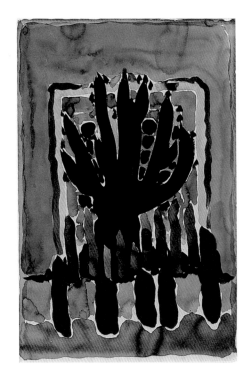

Figure 17
Georgia O'Keeffe
Trees and Picket Fence 1918
Watercolor on paper
17⅞ × 11⅞ in. (45.4 × 30.2 cm)
Collection of the Milwaukee Art Mu-
seum, Gift of Mrs. Harry Lynde Bradley

photograph as a cubist flattening of
space, and O'Keeffe likewise remarked
on his similarity to Picasso.

Within this intense period of contact—a barrage of letters, prints, and
articles from Stieglitz's periodical *Camera Work*—Strand's vision imprinted
itself firmly on O'Keeffe's own. She
moved from "making Strand photographs for myself in my head" to
making them on paper. Several watercolors in this exhibition, rendered by
O'Keeffe with varying degrees of abstraction, suggest a close relationship
to Strand's *White Fence*. In a composition of multiple rectangles (also reminiscent of Dow)—her *Red House with
Fence and Door* (1916–18; fig. 16)—
O'Keeffe explored geometric patterning on an insistently flat surface (this
watercolor is part of *Georgia O'Keeffe:
Canyon Suite*, a distinct exhibition).
Considerably looser is her *Trees and
Picket Fence* (1918; fig. 17), in which
overlapping rows of vertical strokes
create the fence effect; behind it a flattened tree seems compressed into the
shallow space between fence and a
series of framing rectangles—a window or door in the background.

Still, she was not quite finished with
the geometry of fences and windows.
The following spring (1918), while
O'Keeffe was recuperating from the flu

in the San Antonio area, Stieglitz sent Strand to Texas to bring her back to New York. O'Keeffe took several weeks—both difficult and pleasurable, thanks to Strand—to make up her mind about leaving Texas.[53] Stieglitz had sent her a new box of paints, and it was perhaps with those that she rendered *Window—Red and Blue Sill* (1918; cat. 26), yet another variant on rectangles and internal framing. Behind all of these watercolors, lingering as a palimpsest, we can visualize the twin influences of Dow's geometric exercises overlaid with Strand's example in finding abstraction within real-world subjects.

In Texas, besides finding geometric forms in architectural subjects, O'Keeffe sometimes created patterns within the vastness outside her door. In *Abstraction Blue* (1917; cat. 25) she turned a vast, open place into a self-reflexive one by framing a manageable bit of it. Within a horseshoe-shaped band of inky blue, she enclosed a star-sprinkled disk of night sky. Decades later O'Keeffe reopened her Texas experiments in ordering nature—not by reducing it to her own scale, but by imposing a pattern on the vastness. Looking out on clouds from an airplane window, she conceived the notion of painting them. In *Sky Above Clouds III* (1963; cat. 32), O'Keeffe paved heaven with rows of clouds that invite the viewer to imagine walking out across them, beyond where the eye can reach. Within the carefully ordered placement of cloud forms one detects a delicate network of implied diagonals, verticals, and horizontals on a surface that is both flat and deeply spatial. The size of this painting, a substantial four by seven feet, makes it a panorama of light and sky, an infinitude without end. Before she finished, O'Keeffe painted a final work in this series, the massive *Sky Above Clouds IV* (1965, The Art Institute of Chicago, not in exhibition), which measures an astonishing eight by twenty-four feet and becomes a kind of artistic spectacle on the scale of Monet's water lilies, wrapping the viewer in an unearthly surround.

O'Keeffe would use the central organizing principle of the grid, much modified, to study two-dimensional formal relationships in many future works. With great imaginative variety, she extended those inquiries, first at Lake George, then in her New York skyscrapers, and later in New Mexico.

In the 1920s, while summering at Lake George, O'Keeffe often painted the barns and outbuildings near the Stieglitz family compound. One such work is *Red Barn, Lake George, New York* (1921; cat. 27), in which the artist extends the Texas architectural studies into a painting of geometric shapes masquerading as forthright realism. The barn is divided into heavily out-lined shapes: a great dark rectangular door is set within a larger red rectangular wall. That surface, in turn, is surmounted by a prominent triangular gable upon which a dense cloud-band seems to balance. What seems realist here is also assertively abstract—simple but carefully thought out in its divisions of space. The black door, particularly, is a portent of many doors to come.

O'Keeffe painted *Lake George Window* (cat. 28) in 1929, more than a decade after her departure from Texas. In medium (oil) and larger size, the work differs greatly from her Texas water-colors of windows and doors, but we see in it some of the same concerns O'Keeffe had initiated there. A composition of ostensible symmetry and quietude, *Lake George Window* is in fact alive with subtle tensions and calculated imprecision. It is both like and unlike the photographs with which it has often been compared. Originally titled *Portrait of a Farmhouse*, this painting extends the synoptic way O'Keeffe approached many of

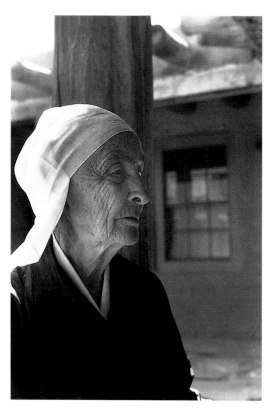

Figure 18
Fritz Kaeser
Georgia O'Keeffe #8 1968
Silver gelatin print
Collection of the Snite Museum of Art,
University of Notre Dame, Gift of Milly
Kaeser

her object-portraits. And, though based on actual buildings, we can scarcely ignore O'Keeffe's reordering of observed reality in such paintings; through her emphasis on relational rectangles she clearly acknowledges the residual design principles (especially the flat black-and-white contrasts of *notan*) absorbed from Dow.

An implicit but unstated grid appears in an unlikely work from these years, *Wave, Night,* discussed above for its curvilinear embrace of land and water. What appear only after long looking are O'Keeffe's spatial divisions: horizontally by the luminous horizon line, almost exactly midway between top and bottom; and vertically by the pin-dot of the lighthouse, precisely centered between the gray and black rectangles that form the painting's upper half.[54] Seen this way, a painting of ostensibly simple, organic shapes is revealed as a disciplined formal exercise, extending O'Keeffe's engagement with Dow's studies of linear harmonies.

In 1929, when O'Keeffe began spending most summers in New Mexico, she was taken with the rough wooden crosses planted in the landscape by the Penitente Brotherhood as part of their ritual Lenten practices. Standing alone, silhouetted against the sky, the crosses suggested the way Catholicism seems planted in the very soil of northern New Mexico. In formal terms, O'Keeffe's cross paintings frame their space-dividing cruciform shapes within rectangles and squares—compositions powerfully reminiscent of Dow's sample exercises in *Composition*. *Gray Cross with Blue* (1929; cat. 29), the most luminous of O'Keeffe's crosses, incorporates the glowing sky she had learned to paint in Texas with a central icon that stands in for the absent light source. Structure and symbol collude to produce meaning: the cross's light-struck horizontal and vertical members silently proclaim the ways in which nature and culture intersect in the New Mexico landscape. O'Keeffe felt the power of her crosses: "For me," she wrote, "painting the crosses was a way of painting the country."[55]

New Mexico's flat-roofed adobe architecture gave O'Keeffe another way of painting the country. The simple cubes of buildings, with proportions often dictated by materials, appealed to O'Keeffe's long-standing reductivist taste while providing many opportunities for her to continue her investigation of geometric patterning. In 1940, the year she purchased a home at Ghost Ranch, New Mexico, she painted *From the Patio I* (cat. 30), an asymmetrical fragment of wall, conspicuous like *Lake George Window* for its tight execution and controlled relational rectangles. It is also a progeny of her San Antonio composition *Window—Red and Blue Sill:* again, the window is the focal point, but at Ghost Ranch its gridded form contains a complex reflection from an adjacent wall. O'Keeffe would refine this spare geometry for nearly a half-century in New Mexico. We see her photographed, perhaps against this very window, by Fritz Kaeser in 1968 (fig. 18).

Later in the 1940s O'Keeffe restored a ruined New Mexico adobe house in the village of Abiquiu, not far from Ghost Ranch. It was a house she said she bought for its black patio door, and she proceeded to paint that door with insistence. In all seasons and weathers she recorded its shape, punctuating the otherwise featureless adobe wall. Mostly she painted it as one saw it—an inky black. But sometimes she experimented with color, as in *Wall with Green Door* (1952; cat. 31). Here the pale green rectangle floats, slightly off-center, against the warm tan wall expanse. Only its deeper shading toward the top suggests the door's recession within the wall, a single whisper

of depth in a painting of otherwise unrelieved flatness. A painter without O'Keeffe's long experience in distilling observed forms could not have pulled it off: a composition of horizontal ribbons, minimalist, yet not abstract.

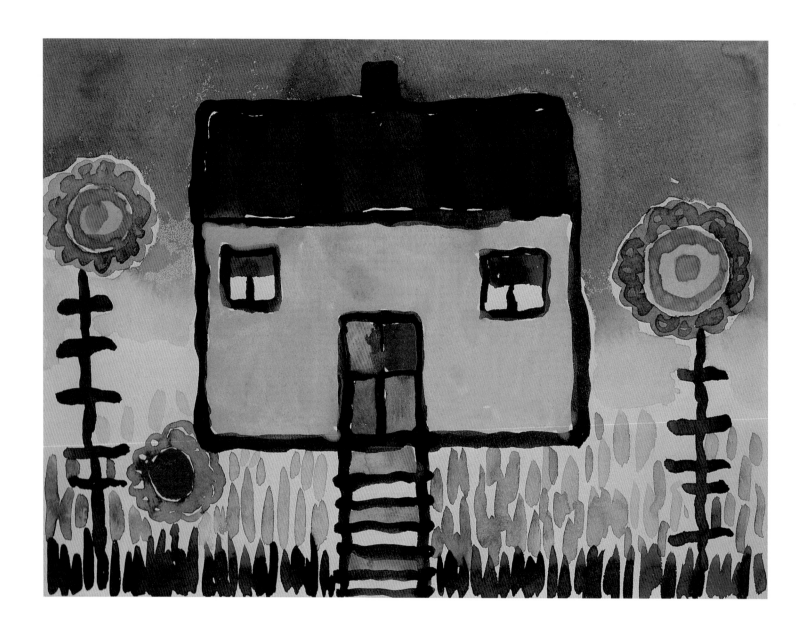

Geometric Patterns/21
Yellow House
1917
Watercolor
The Gerald Peters Gallery

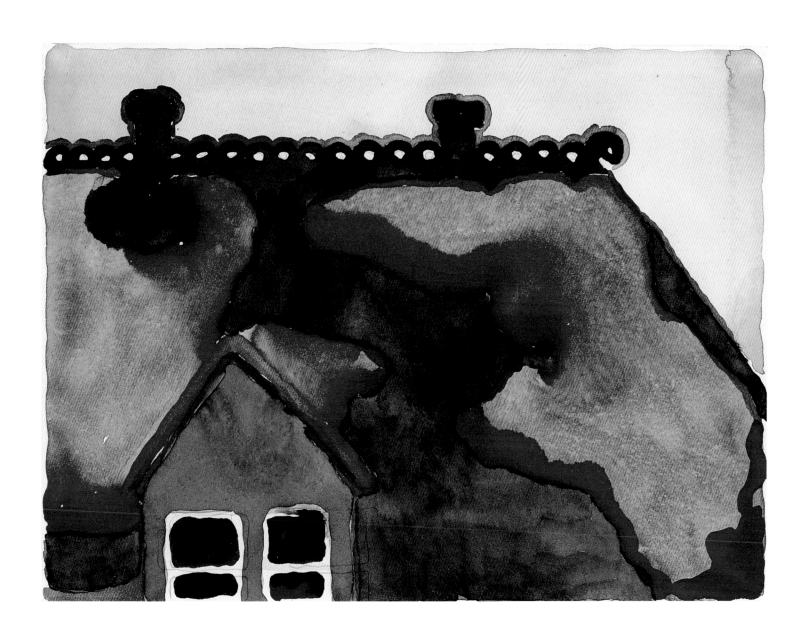

Geometric Patterns/22
Roof with Snow
1917
Watercolor on paper
Amarillo Museum of Art

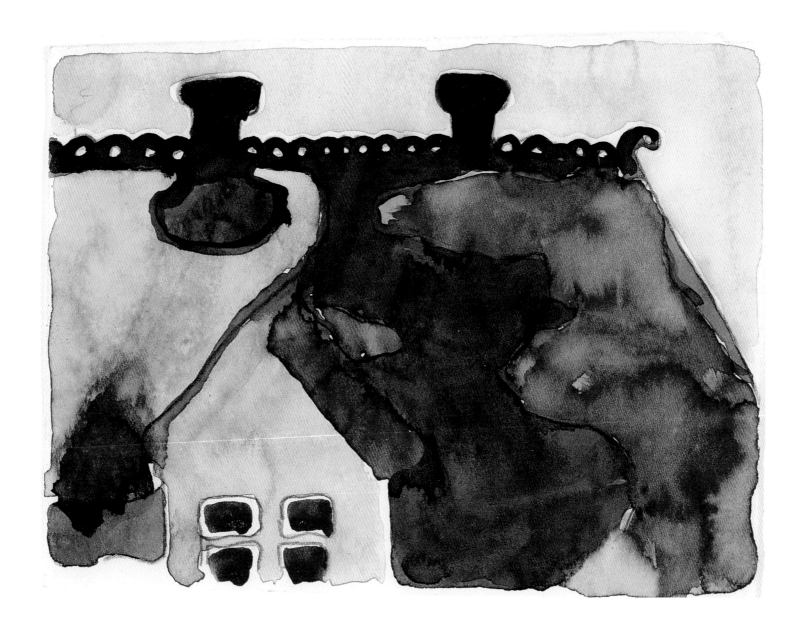

Geometric Patterns/23
Roof with Snow—Study Sketch
1917
Watercolor on paper
Amarillo Museum of Art

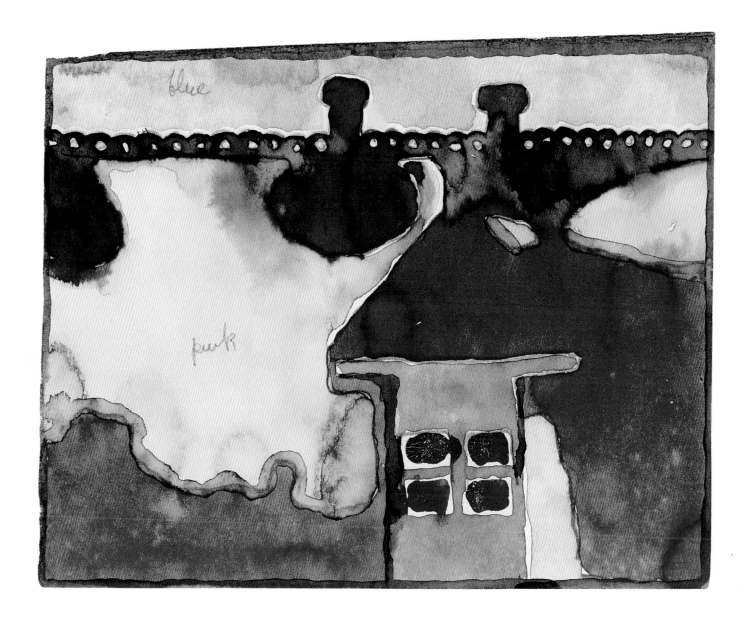

Geometric Patterns/24
Roof with Snow—Study Sketch
1917
Watercolor on paper
Amarillo Museum of Art

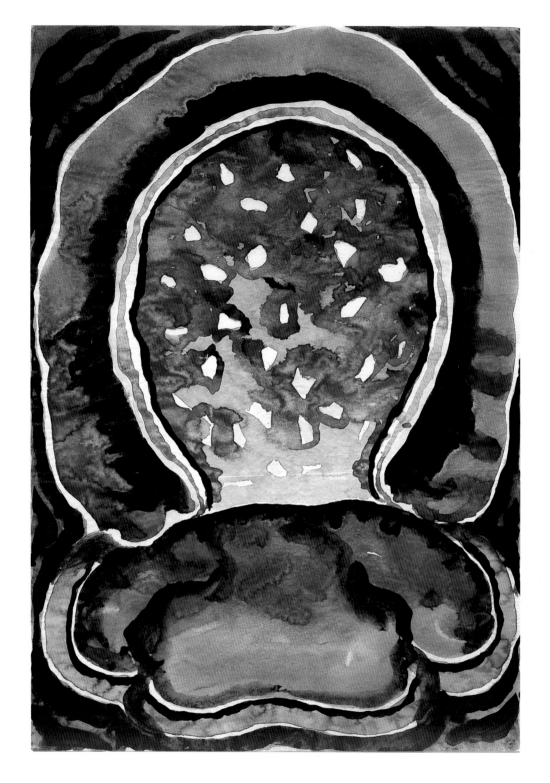

Geometric Patterns/25
Abstraction Blue
1917
Watercolor
The Gerald Peters Gallery

Geometric Patterns/26
Window—Red and Blue Sill
1918
Watercolor on paper
Georgia O'Keeffe Museum

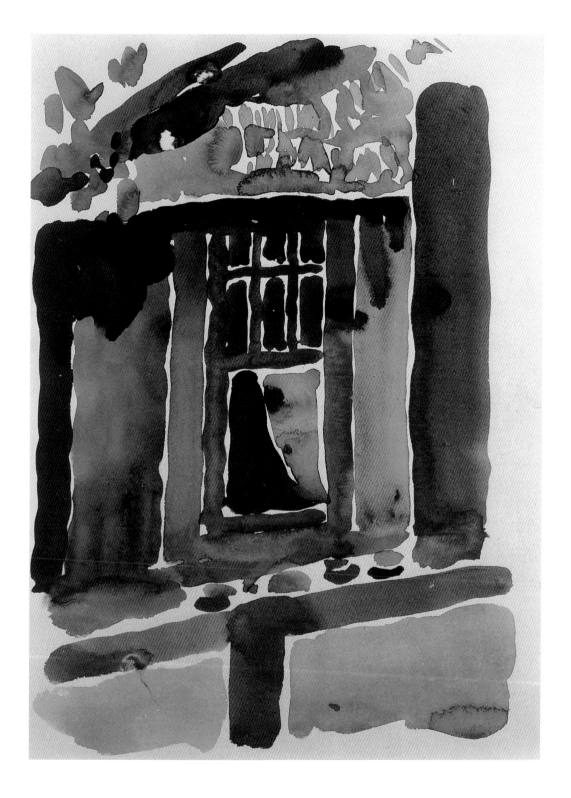

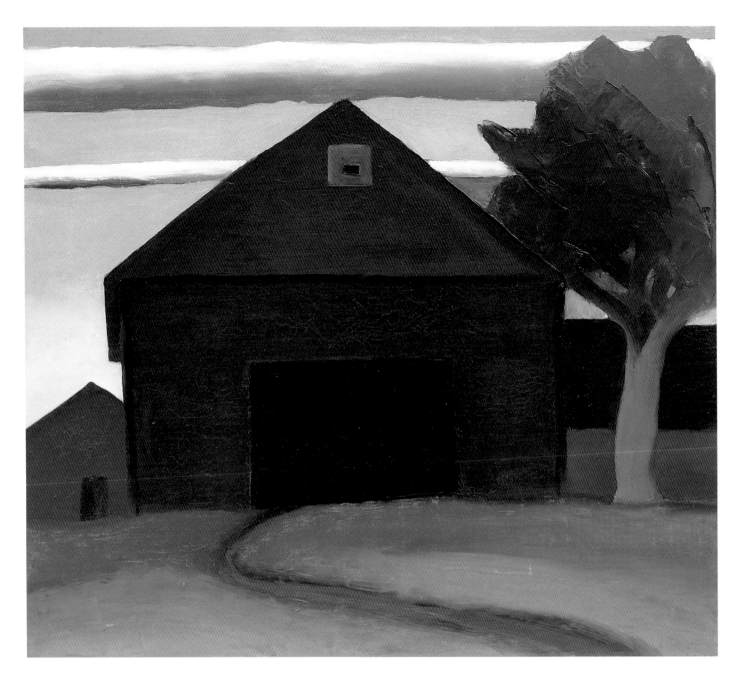

Geometric Patterns/27
Red Barn, Lake George, New York
1921
Oil on canvas
Georgia Museum of Art, University of Georgia

Geometric Patterns/28
Lake George Window
1929
Oil on canvas
The Museum of Modern Art

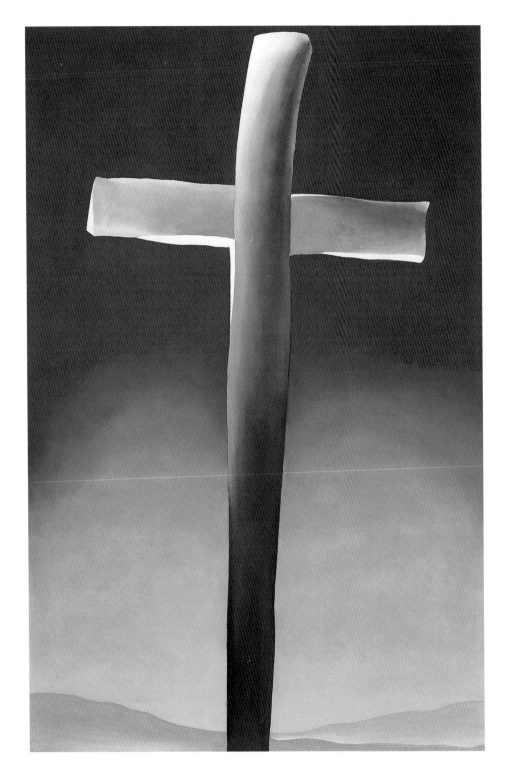

"For me, painting the crosses was a way of painting the country."

Geometric Patterns/29
Gray Cross with Blue
1929
Oil on canvas
The Albuquerque Museum

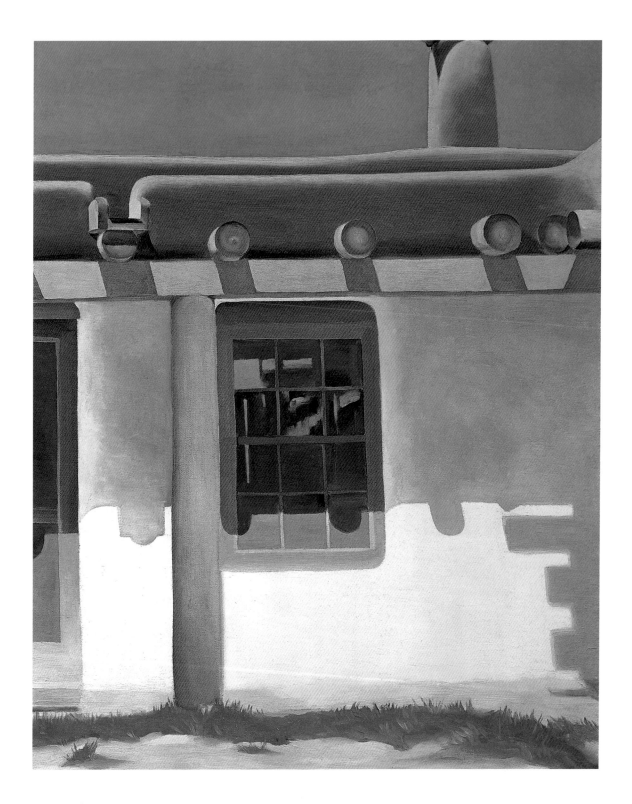

Geometric Patterns/30
From the Patio I
1940
Oil on canvas
The Gerald Peters Gallery

Geometric Patterns/31
Wall with Green Door
1952
Oil on canvas
The Corcoran Gallery of Art

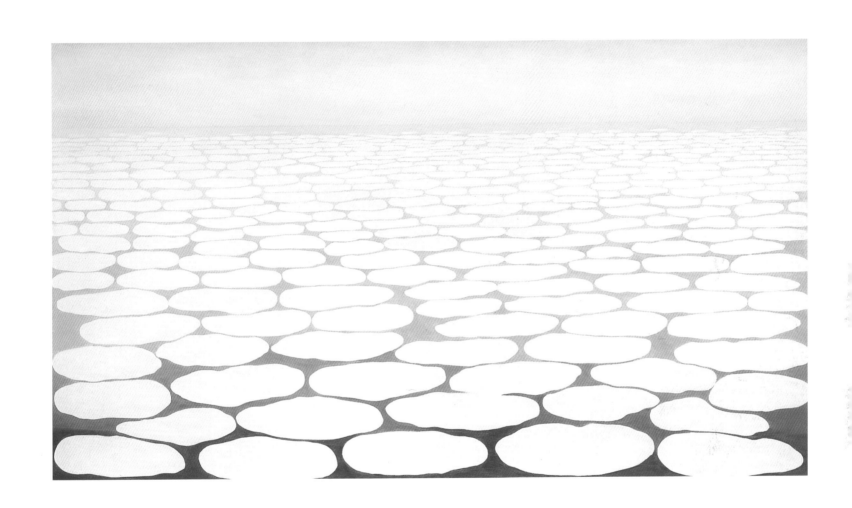

Geometric Patterns/32
Sky Above Clouds III
1963
Oil on canvas
Private Collection

Solids and Voids: Nature's spectacle in Texas and beyond

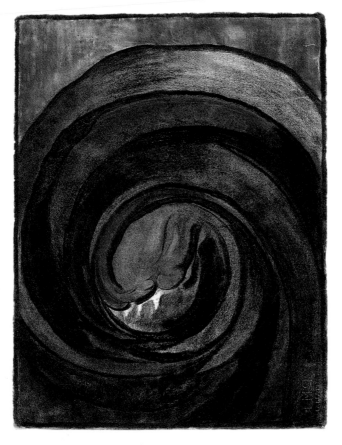

Figure 19
Georgia O'Keeffe
Drawing No. 8 1915
Charcoal on paper mounted on
cardboard
24¼ × 18⅞ in. (61.6 × 47.9 cm)
Collection of the Whitney Museum of
American Art, New York, Purchase, with
funds from the Mr. and Mrs. Arthur G.
Altschul Purchase Fund

The nights in Canyon were exceptionally quiet, except for the sound of lowing cattle or the occasional train whistle. O'Keeffe wrote about those nighttime trains: "The night very still—a train way off rumbling and humming Ive heard it a long time—I dont know whether it is coming or going I guess its coming."[56] Sometimes she got up to watch the train arrive, and afterward recorded the effects on paper. She made several watercolors of the remembered image, each emphasizing the great clouds of smoke spewing from the engine. In *Train Coming In—Canyon, Texas* (1918; cat. 34), the tiny locomotive is nearly lost beneath the clouds swelling against the edges of the page. This is a composition based on curves; arcing tracks at the lower left sweep through the nexus of the tiny locomotive into vast oppositional curves describing the cloud. This watercolor in turn recalls one of O'Keeffe's free, abstract charcoals, *Drawing No. 8* (1915; fig. 19), an inward coil expressive of great centripetal energies.

Closely related to those images is a

series of watercolors O'Keeffe began in 1916—paintings that reintroduce color after her self-imposed restriction to charcoal. The great coil or spiral contained within *Blue I* (ca. 1917; cat. 33) seems to grow directly out of O'Keeffe's studies in charcoal and watercolor, and to relate to the expansive circular forms in the train watercolors. Her reintroduction of color, as has been widely shown, was spurred by her reading of the influential Russian-born theorist Wassily Kandinsky, whose *Concerning the Spiritual in Art* O'Keeffe had already studied twice by 1916. Kandinsky urged his readers to harken to their own "inner necessity" and to use color with recognition of its specific attributes and powers. O'Keeffe's experiments with blue, as in *Blue I,* follow Kandinsky's assertion that blue tends to turn in upon its own center, expressing profound meaning, depth, and coolness. Stieglitz photographed O'Keeffe's hands in front of one of her Blue series paintings from 1917 (fig. 20), an indication that both felt it an important one.

When O'Keeffe returned later to the expressive potential of blue, it was sometimes in a similarly abstract fashion. As Kandinsky had argued, "The more abstract is form, the more clear and direct is its appeal."[57] One such example is O'Keeffe's *Abstraction, Blue* (1927; cat. 38), a painting whose bifurcated swelling forms seem related to at least four other O'Keeffe subjects: her contemporaneous delicate flower paintings; the axial symmetry of such works as *Lake George;* the great clouds generated by Texas trains; and, as we shall see, to other sky-events on the Texas plains. Turned ninety degrees to vertical, the format of *Abstraction, Blue* belies its relationship to landscape; but that partial rotation is something O'Keeffe would often do, as if to test the validity of her composition (important in Japanese aesthetics and, subsequently, in abstract photographs) from any orientation.[58] We see it once more in *Blue I* (1958; cat. 45), in which the broad bands of color are apparently based on the sky layerings she saw during her air travels of those later years. Yet the composition has been

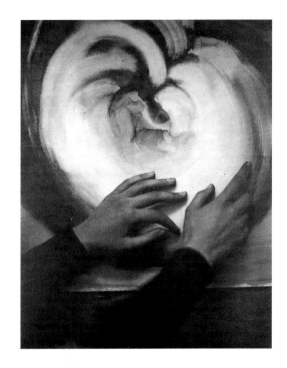

Figure 20
Alfred Stieglitz
Georgia O'Keeffe: A Portrait—Hands and Watercolor, June 4, 1917 1917
Platinum photograph
National Gallery of Art, Washington, D.C., Alfred Stieglitz Collection

rotated to vertical, with a wisp of cloud dragged diagonally across. Again, the suggestion is of strongly Japanese influence.

Still another painting that seems to employ axial rotation to press toward abstraction is *Pink Abstraction* (1929; cat. 40), another hybrid of multiple concerns dating back at least a decade to O'Keeffe's Texas work. Here the great perimeter arcs split by a banded vertical wedge strongly recall the great Texas sky-arcs, especially if considered horizontally. But this painting registers monumentality simultaneously with intimacy. Even as it evokes landscape references, *Pink Abstraction*'s tender coloration and its delicate wavelike forms conjure up a kinship to the soft, folding forms within the clam shells and sweetpeas O'Keeffe painted in 1926 and 1927. Her *Iris (Dark Iris No. 1)* (1927; cat. 39) belongs as well to these studies of divided circularity; within its shallow space the iris bloom undulates gently, its folded petals in dialogue with a number of O'Keeffe's homologous abstractions from those years.

The raw sensory data she received in Texas stimulated O'Keeffe's painting in many other ways. Perhaps it was Stieglitz's friend William Carlos Williams who inspired her to use all her faculties to express place. In 1915

Williams had written, "I will express my emotions in the appearances: surface, sounds, smells, touch of the place in which I happen to be."[59] What Williams formulated in words, O'Keeffe translated into a poetics for the eye. In the city, competing sensory impressions might dull the impact of each. But in West Texas the immense vacuum of the night allowed O'Keeffe to sort out the sounds, smells, and textures of objects made distinct from each other by the dark void. As she walked out onto the plains, she could experience each sensation's source in nature, without the contextuality imposed by daylight. Her nighttime imaginings, abetted by isolated lights and sound cues, encouraged the artist to abstract and invent from the natural incident.

Besides the sound of the train whistle, another powerful auditory experience was provided by the vast herds of cattle that regularly passed through the Panhandle towns. Raising enormous dust clouds on the move, or lowing in their pens at night, they stirred O'Keeffe's imagination in new ways. She had known it since her first arrival in Texas: she recalled that "In my Amarillo days cows had been so much a part of the country I couldn't think of it without them."[60] Later, at

Canyon, the lowing cattle made what seemed to her a new form of sound: "I like it—and I don't like it—it's like music—I made up a tune to it this morning," she wrote.[61] Over time, the haunting bovine music of the Texas herds fused in her imagination with the plaintive folk songs of the region, which had the same sad, keening quality.

The cattle in the pens lowing for their calves day and night was a sound that has always haunted me. It had a regular rhythmic beat like the old Penitente songs, repeating the same rhythms over and over all through the day and night. It was loud and raw under the stars in that wide empty country.[62]

A sometime musician herself (she had once studied piano and had struggled for several years to teach herself violin), O'Keeffe developed an expansive, flexible definition of music. In her classes at Columbia, O'Keeffe had learned to express in drawings the sounds she heard on records. Now, in Texas, she found that nature's own music could inspire images for the eye. The idea of sensory crossovers—synesthesia—was an idea much talked about by American and European artists early in the century.[63] In Dow's thinking, music—the most abstract of the arts—was the ideal model for those seeking visual abstraction.

A painting O'Keeffe made following her departure from Canyon relates some of the visual shapes and monumentality of Texas to the expressive qualities of music. In *Blue and Green Music* (1919; cat. 35), loose wavelike and flamelike shapes, interspersed with dark-toned linear bands, suggest the unconventional rhythms arising in nature. Dissonant in form, unified in color, *Blue and Green Music* is a visual composition of distinctly modern harmonies.

The energies and cloudlike forms in *Blue and Green Music*, as well as those in *Abstraction, Blue* and *Pink Abstraction*, recall still another aspect of sensory stimulation O'Keeffe encountered on the Texas plains. There, on the endless canvas of the sky, weather paraded its effects. Storms, seen approaching from far off, ignited vast sections of the sky; these kicked off performances of sound and light unmatched in O'Keeffe's experience. To Anita Pollitzer, O'Keeffe wrote from Canyon of a sky ablaze with visual incident: "the whole thing—lit up—first in one place—then in another with flashes of lightning—sometimes just sheet lightning—and sometimes sheet lightning with a sharp bright zigzag flash-

ing across—I . . . sat on the fence for a long time—just looking at the lightning—"[64]

From that long looking came vivid memories of nature's great sky abstractions. In 1919 O'Keeffe painted *Orange and Red Streak* (1919; cat. 36), in which two great arcs of light joined by a zigzag seem a close parallel to O'Keeffe's own description quoted above.

Years later, O'Keeffe's Texas friend Ted Reid remembered her rapt attentiveness to dramatic weather: "Did you ever see her watch a great storm? There was never anyone in the world like her in her appreciation of such things."[65] O'Keeffe remembered, too, for some thirty-five years later she revisited the visual sky spectacle she had encountered on the Texas plains. *From the Plains I* (1953; cat. 44) demonstrates that O'Keeffe had forgotten neither the sound nor the lightning's jagged shapes nor the searing hot color that were all part of her Texas experience.

When lightning swept its abstract calligraphy across the sky, it created shapes that suggested both solids and voids. From the great arcs of lightning and from the swirling shapes within storm clouds, O'Keeffe derived certain favored shapes she would use repeatedly. Ovoid or circular forms, redis-

covered in countless objects, became some of O'Keeffe's signature shapes. We have already seen them in such paintings as *Lake George with Crows*. In *Leaf Motif* #2 (1924; cat. 37), O'Keeffe layered oak leaves one over another, the large voids between their lobes as significant as the solid shapes.

Later she would seek out similar relationships between solids and voids in, for example, animal bones. O'Keeffe's interest in animal bones began in Texas, where she found them on the plains near Amarillo and brought them into her classroom for students to see. When she encountered cattle skulls and other bones again in New Mexico, it was like coming across familiar, well-loved forms. She picked them up, admired their bleached whiteness, and held them up to the cerulean expanse of sky. Instead of death, they suggested life to her: she remarked famously that

The bones seem to cut sharply to the center of something that is keenly alive on the desert even tho' it is vast and empty and untouchable— and knows no kindness with all its beauty.[66]

When she painted *Pelvis with Blue (Pelvis I)* (1944; cat. 42), O'Keeffe combined solids and voids in ways that engage the viewer in visual play: held up against the sky, which are the solid forms, which the negative spaces?

The following year, as if in three-dimensional dialogue with the pelvis paintings, O'Keeffe produced one of her rare sculptures, a work called *Abstraction*, which she later had cast in several sizes and materials (1945, cast 1980; cat. 43). It seems a natural outgrowth of the three-dimensional abstraction often suggested in her paintings, characterized by luminous color and strong modeling. *Abstraction* extends in three dimensions what she had often done in two: enclosing a circular void with a spiraling line, a line itself expanded to become shape.

That spiraling line in *Abstraction* recalls O'Keeffe's many other ventures into the expansive possibilities of the spiral. They had begun early, emerging from germinal early charcoals such as *Drawing No. 8*, and continuing in Texas with *Blue I* (cat. 33) and the rolling rings of light in *Evening Star, No. V.* Later, in typical O'Keeffe fashion, she found the spiraling line manifested in natural forms. Shells, in particular, allowed O'Keeffe to cross over again from abstraction into realism. Over the years she picked up shells on many beaches of the world and brought them to her studio. Eventually she painted them both in and out of con-

text: she tried them with seaweed, old shingles, spiky coral. She situated them in isolation and in groups. Among her most compelling shells are several enormously magnified ones painted against a red hill, from 1938 (see *Red Hills with White Shell*, cat. 41). Here the shell's size and decontextualization cast it instantly into some otherworldly realm. As we stare fixedly, the spiraling line sweeps us into, then out from, the center. Against its preternaturally still backdrop, which approaches the surreal in its disquieting intensity, the shell form becomes mesmerizing, like a vivid, dizzying dream. The dream simile is a useful one, for spirals have often been cited as images of dreams and self-discovery. Carl Jung, whom O'Keeffe read at several points in her life, found that the process of self-discovery

is not straight but appears to go round in circles. More accurate knowledge has proved it to go in spirals: the dream-motifs always return after certain intervals to definite forms, whose characteristic it is to define a centre. . . . the process of development proves on closer inspection to be cyclic or spiral.[67]

O'Keeffe's paintings of shells are paradoxical images of expansion and enclosure, of voyages out and journeys of return. In this they accord perfectly

with the path of O'Keeffe's creative development, always drawing time and experience back into the widening sphere of her visual expression. Rather than abandoning her early forms, she returned again and again to the centering images through which she understood her own relationship to the natural world.

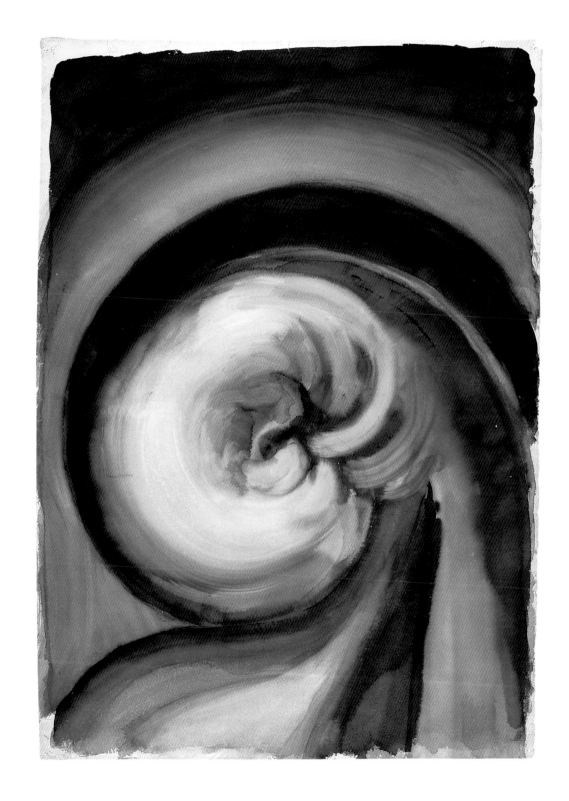

Solids and Voids/33
Blue I
ca.1917
Watercolor on paper
Robert L. B. Tobin

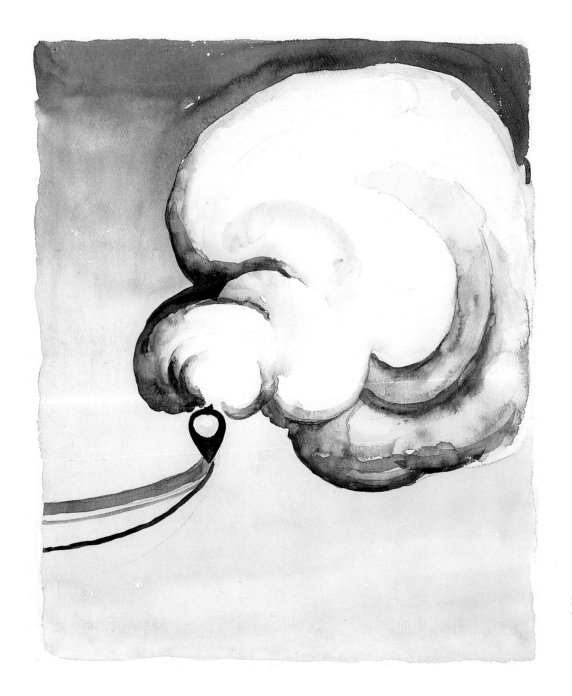

Solids and Voids/34
Train Coming In—Canyon, Texas
1918
Watercolor on paper
Amarillo Museum of Art

Solids and Voids/35
Blue and Green Music
1919
Oil on canvas
The Art Institute of Chicago

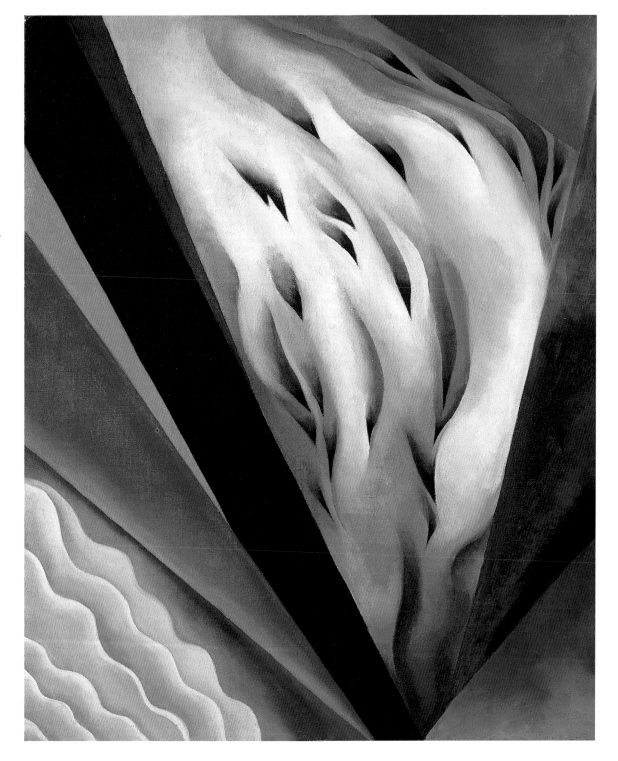

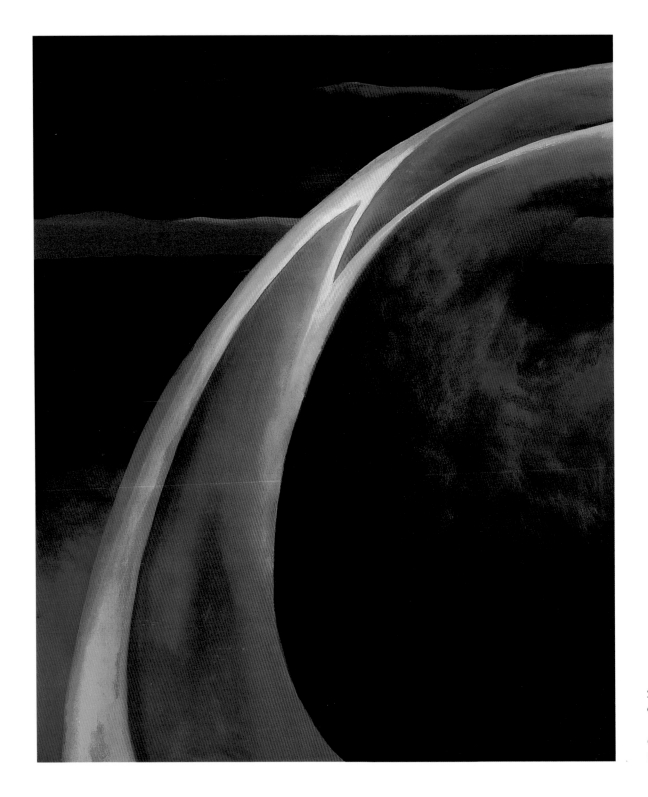

Solids and Voids/36
Orange and Red Streak
1919
Oil on canvas
Philadelphia Museum of Art

Solids and Voids/37
Leaf Motif #2
1924
Oil on canvas
The McNay Art Museum

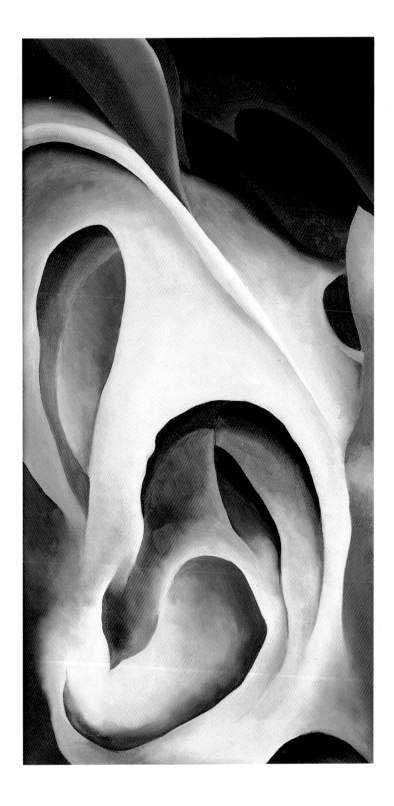

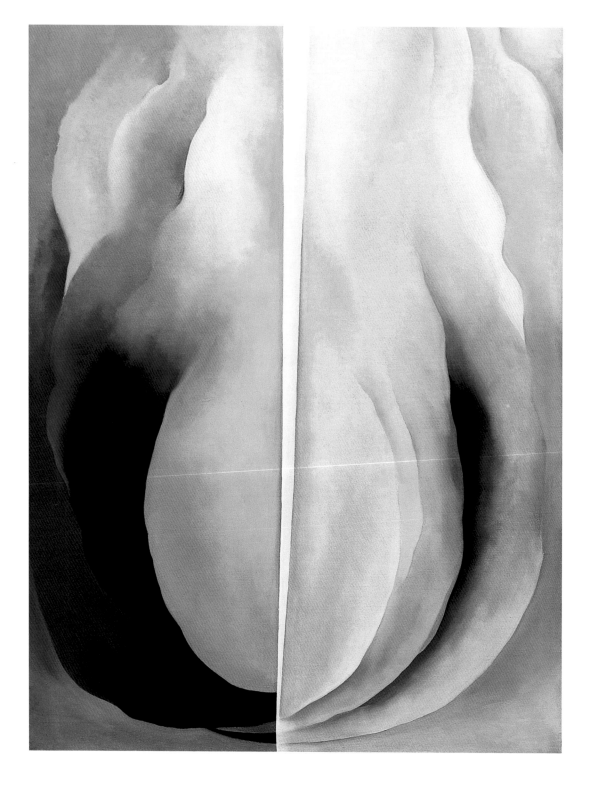

Solids and Voids/38
Abstraction, Blue
1927
Oil on canvas
The Museum of Modern Art

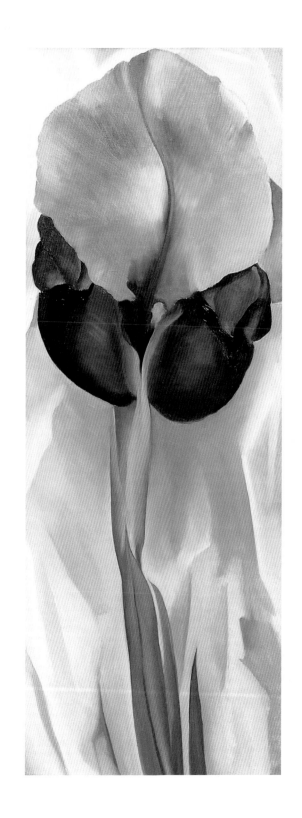

Solids and Voids/39
Iris (Dark Iris No. 1)
1927
Oil on canvas
Colorado Springs Fine Arts Center

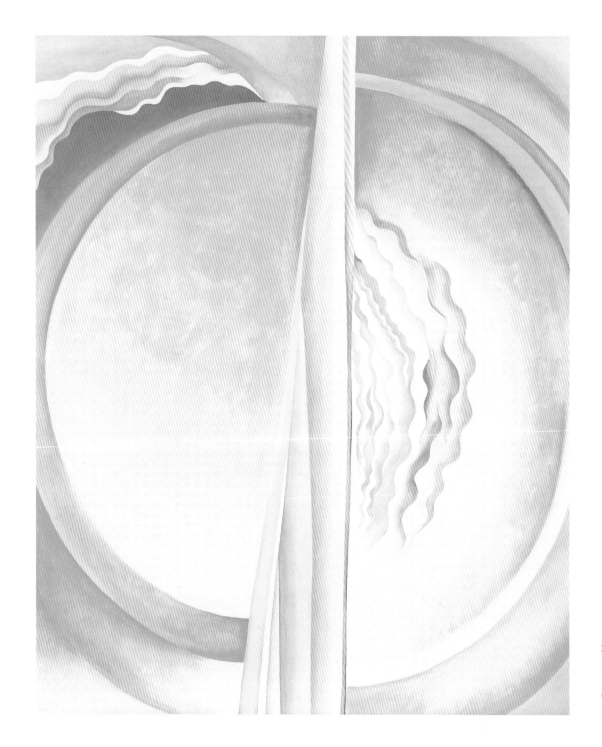

Solids and Voids/40
Pink Abstraction
1929
Oil on canvas
Phoenix Art Museum

Solids and Voids/41
Red Hills with White Shell
1938
Oil on canvas
The Museum of Fine Arts, Houston

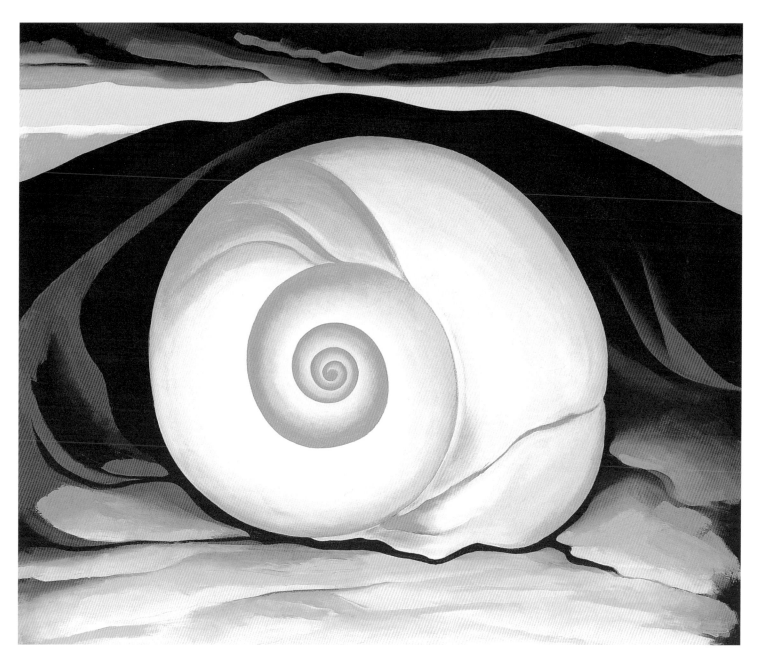

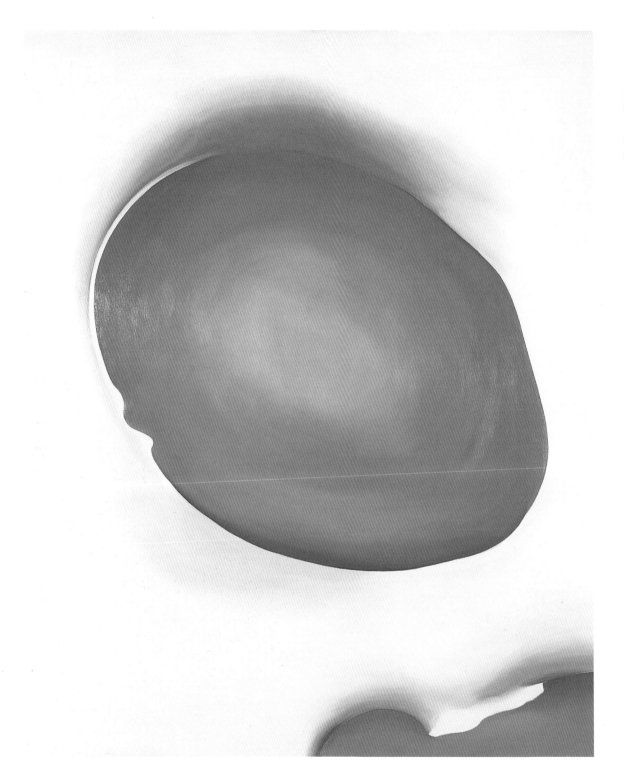

Solids and Voids/42
Pelvis with Blue (Pelvis I)
1944
Oil on canvas
Milwaukee Art Museum

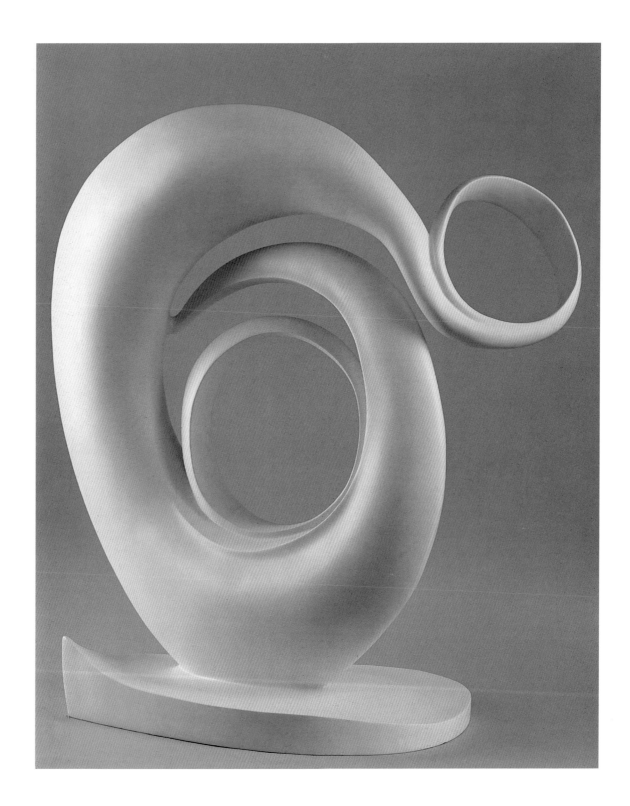

Solids and Voids/43
Abstraction
1945, cast 1980
White lacquered bronze
The Gerald Peters Gallery

89

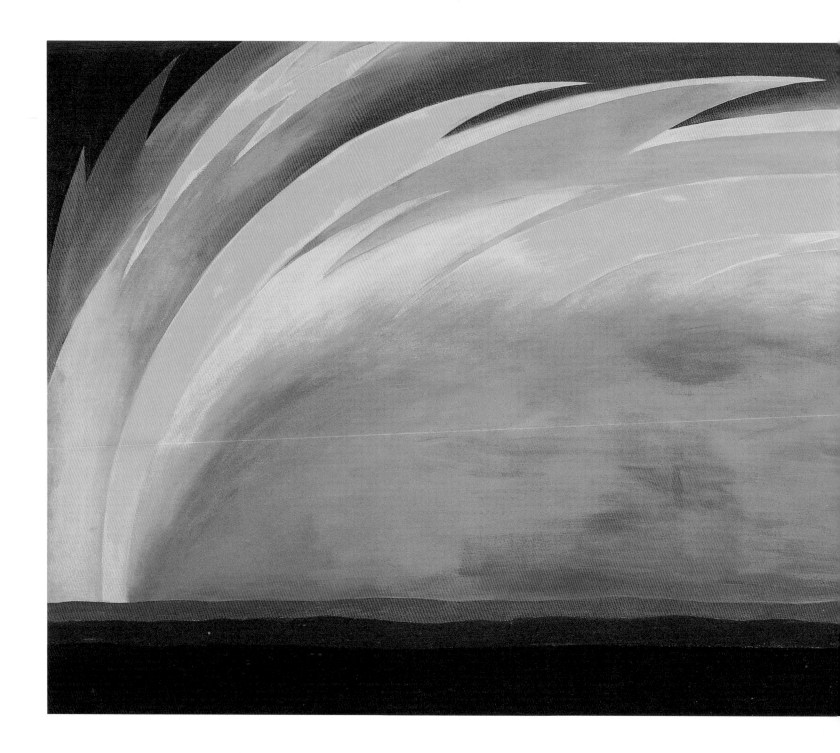

"I . . . sat on the fence for a long time—just looking at the lightning—"

Solids and Voids/44
From the Plains I
1953
Oil on canvas
The McNay Art Museum

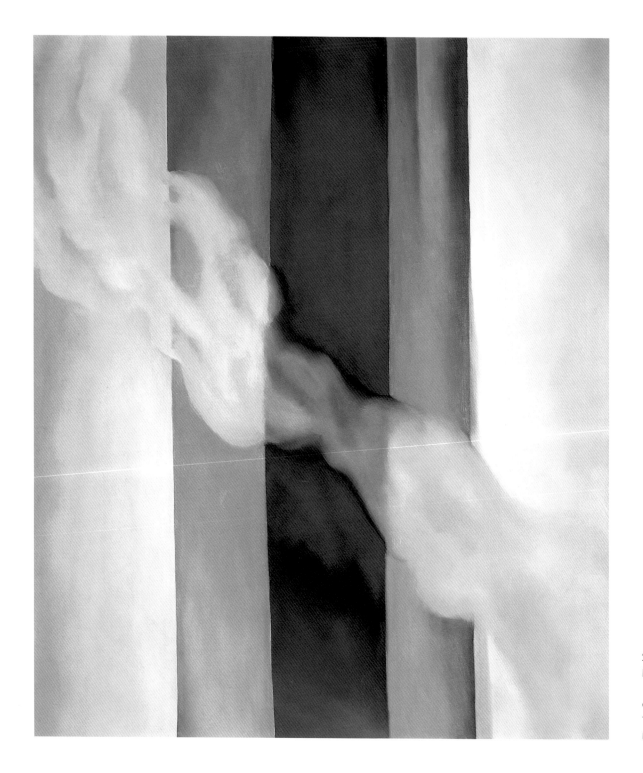

Solids and Voids/45
Blue I
1958
Oil on canvas
The Snite Museum of Art,
University of Notre Dame

Lines: Nature's tracings

The lines O'Keeffe traced in shells and other natural objects held powerful expressive potential, some of which she discovered during her Texas years. Dow's encouragement to use Japanese brush and ink had led to spare linear compositions drawn in straight lines; these works, in charcoal and watercolor, culminated in a series of delicately paired calligraphic lines from 1916. *Blue Lines X* (1916; fig. 21) exemplifies that direction. Even earlier, O'Keeffe had employed the curving, sinuous lines of Art Nouveau in a number of her charcoal Specials from 1915, including *Special No. 2* (fig. 22). In Texas, where the theories she had studied collided with fresh sensations from nature, O'Keeffe pressed her study of lines to new expressive heights. Some were drawn with a fine brush, others created by the unpainted seam between dark color areas. In a Texas watercolor called *Abstraction, Black and Blue* (*Georgia O'Keeffe Canyon Suite*, 1995 ed., plate 14), lines join and descend sinuously through the composition. She revisited this idea about seven years later in *Dark Abstraction*

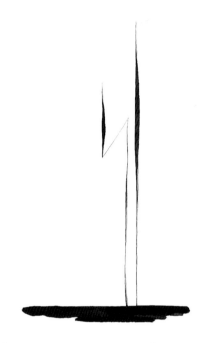

Figure 21
Georgia O'Keeffe
Blue Lines X 1916
Watercolor on paper
25 × 19 in. (63.5 × 48.3 cm)
The Metropolitan Museum of Art, New York, Alfred Stieglitz Collection, 1969

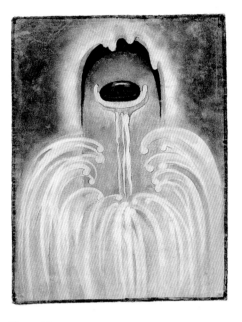

Figure 22
Georgia O'Keeffe
Special No. 2 1915
Charcoal on paper
22 1/16 × 18 1/8 in. (56 × 46 cm)
National Gallery of Art, Washington, D.C., Alfred Stieglitz Collection, Gift of The Georgia O'Keeffe Foundation

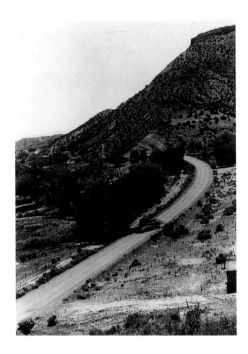

Figure 23
Georgia O'Keeffe
Looking from Bedroom at Abiquiu Towards Española, New Mexico ca. 1955
Silver gelatin print
The Metropolitan Museum of Art, New York, Anonymous Gift, 1977

(1924; cat. 46). When O'Keeffe reproduced this latter painting in her own 1976 book, she downplayed conventional distinctions between the objective and the abstract: "Objective painting," she wrote, "is not good painting unless it is good in the abstract sense. A hill or tree cannot make a good painting just because it is a hill or a tree. It is lines and colors put together so that they say something. For me that is the very basis of painting."[68] Lines, as a vital element in O'Keeffe's abstractions from nature, helped her to draw forth that formal structure in all her compositions. We see it again in later linear paintings, including those based on rivers and roads.

In her Texas paintings of trains O'Keeffe had used the railroad track as the basis for strong, curving linear elements. Five decades later she looked at another human-constructed ribbon— the road stretching out below her bedroom window in the village of Abiquiu. Roads signify human connections, lines between points of origin and destination. This road O'Keeffe knew well. As it swept southward, the road's great curve joined her tranquil village existence with, as she wrote, "Espanola, Santa Fe and the world."[69] Whatever its symbolic connective

value, that glinting ribbon was at least as interesting to her in form as in association. First she photographed it, angling the camera so as to see all of the road. In those photographs the road seemed to stand up, becoming a new shape independent of the earth (see fig. 23). That line, expanding and narrowing sinuously along its course, structures *Road Past the View* (1964; cat. 49) and the even more calligraphic *Winter Road I* (1963; cat. 48).

Rivers also trace linear paths through O'Keeffe's landscape. In *From the River—Light Blue* (1964; cat. 50), O'Keeffe broadened the slow descending liquid curve into a shape of its own. Alongside that wide blue ribbon she introduced a sharp V-shaped element, a reminder of the twin lines she had drawn a half-century earlier in *Blue Lines X*. In *It Was Yellow and Pink II* (1959; cat. 47), a great zigzag of pink line, perhaps based again on the fluvial vitality of a river system seen from the air, is cropped in every direction, framing a whole series of loose triangles within its angular meandering. O'Keeffe's reprise of such linear designs testifies not only to her fidelity to line as a formal element, but to her remarkably consistent artistic vision.

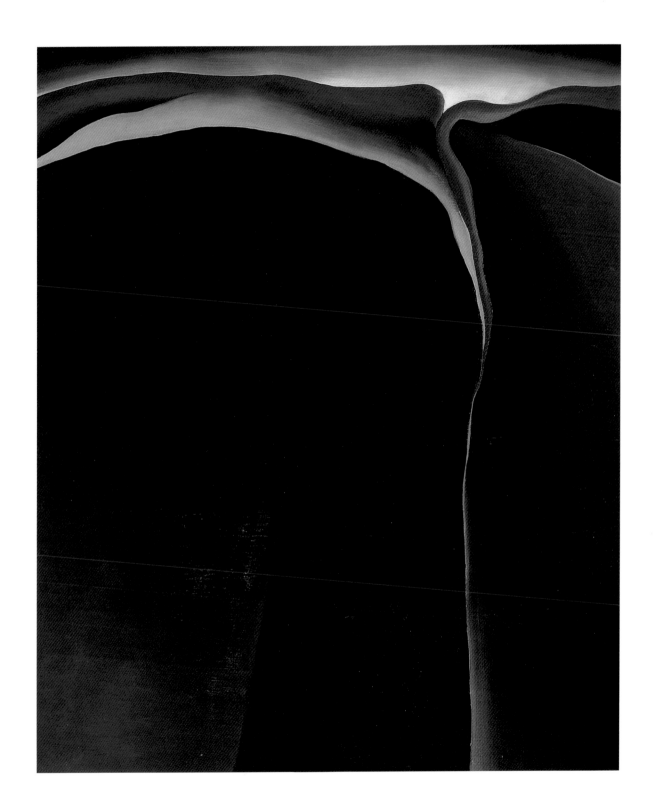

Lines/46
Dark Abstraction
1924
Oil on canvas
The Saint Louis Art
Museum

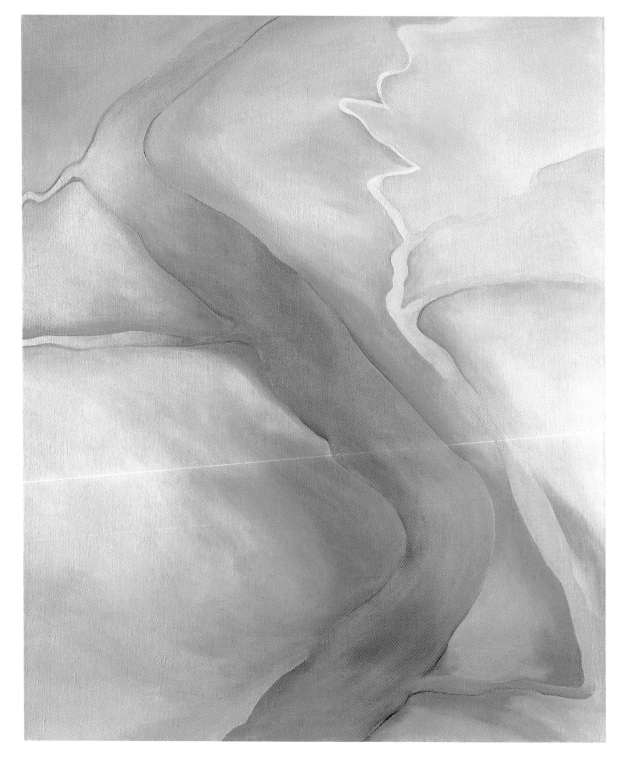

Lines/47
It Was Yellow and Pink II
1959
Oil on canvas
The Cleveland Museum
of Art

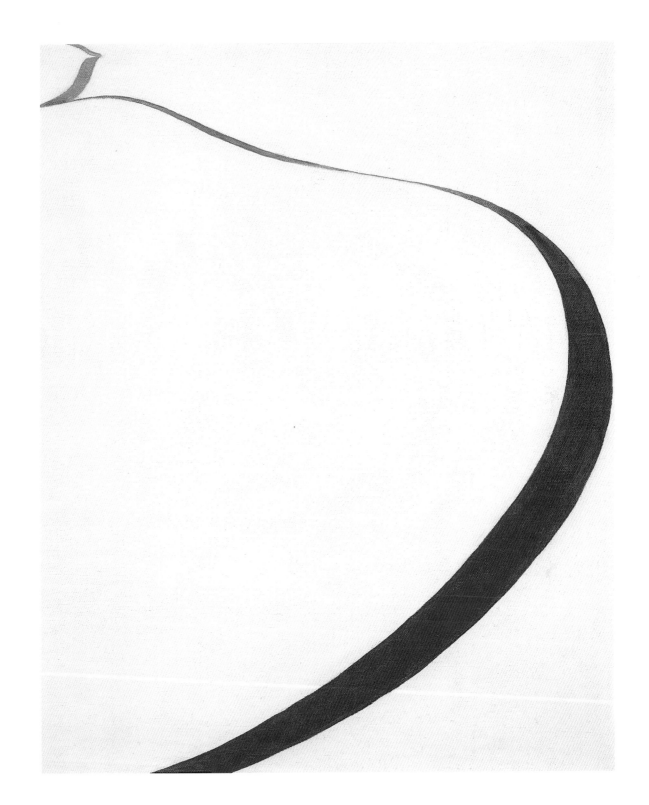

Lines/48
Winter Road I
1963
Oil on canvas
National Gallery of Art

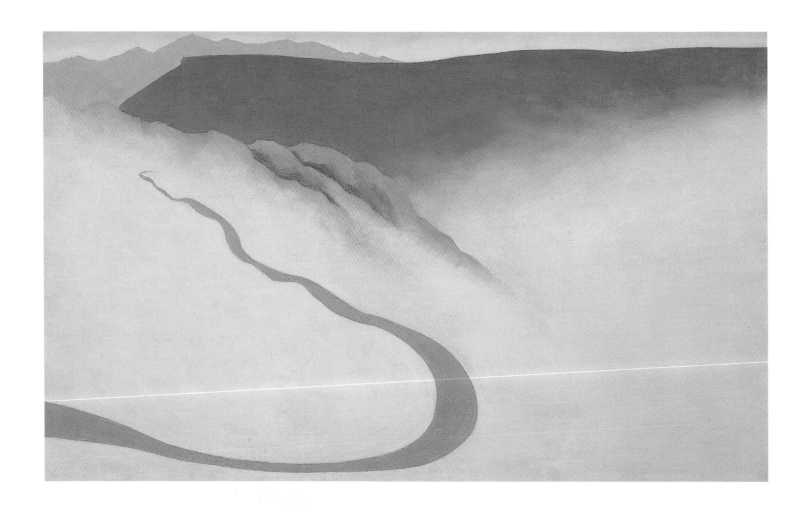

Lines/49
Road Past the View
1964
Oil on canvas
Private Collection

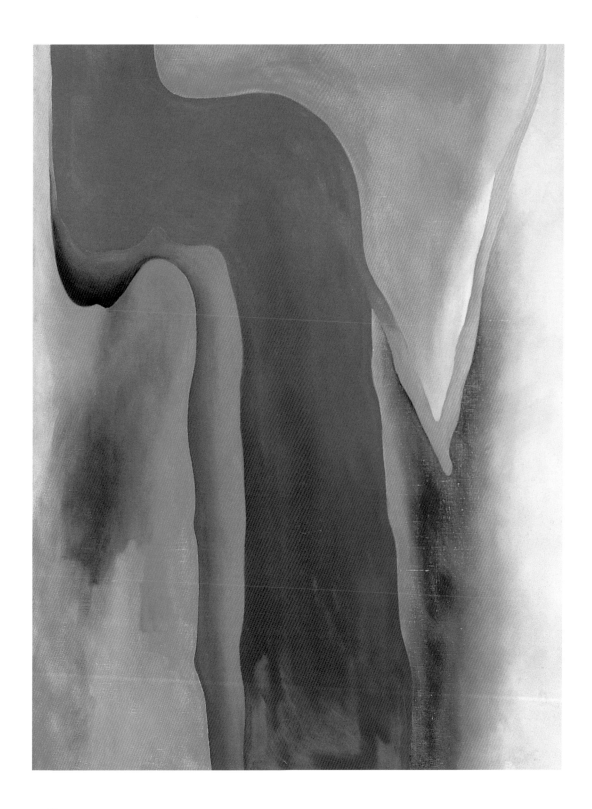

Lines/50
From the River—Light Blue
1964
Oil on canvas
Museum of Fine Arts, Museum of
New Mexico

Conclusion

While teaching at Canyon, O'Keeffe entered her thirties, a woman increasingly confident of her own identity and abilities (fig. 24). What she was less certain about was a place to live; during her years in Texas, Georgia O'Keeffe felt the twin attractions of city and solitude. She could not have them both at the same time, but she arranged not to abandon either one. Teaching in Texas gave her the advantages of space, isolation, and the freedom to create. At the same time she maintained close ties to the East, principally through Anita Pollitzer, her close friend and confidante from the Art Students League. It was Pollitzer who early in 1916 took a roll of O'Keeffe's large charcoal drawings to Alfred Stieglitz, photographer, friend to many artists, and champion of the new modernist ideas. Impressed by O'Keeffe's inventiveness and artistic courage, Stieglitz wrote her voluminous letters filled with encouragement; through their correspondence a deepening friendship was forming throughout her stay at Canyon.

O'Keeffe relied on these two city friends to keep her in touch with New York's art world. Through them she obtained current and back issues of many publications: Stieglitz's *Camera Work*, the *New Republic*, and Charlotte Perkins Gilman's feminist periodical the *Forerunner*. She kept abreast of social issues through the *Masses*, and tackled solid literary works as well: Ibsen and Nietzsche, and Dante's *Divine Comedy*. All this along with her heavy engagement with the aesthetic writings discussed above.

O'Keeffe also began to show her work in New York during the years she spent in Texas. While at Amarillo she exhibited a watercolor, *Scarlet Sage*, in the 1915 American Water Color Society show in New York. Two of her 1915 charcoals—abstractions she titled *Expression No. 14* (later known as *Drawing No. 12*) and *Expression No. 24* were included in the 1917 Independents Show in New York. That same year a Texas watercolor, *Train at Night in the Desert*, became her first sale, purchased for $400 by a private collector from her show at Stieglitz's gallery 291.

Finally, O'Keeffe's efforts to main-

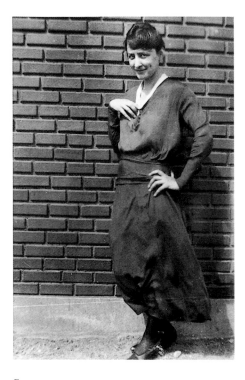

Figure 24
Georgia O'Keeffe at Canyon, Texas
1916 or 1917
Silver gelatin print
Courtesy of The Georgia O'Keeffe
Foundation

tain close ties with New York included her hasty train trip to New York in May 1917, during which she extended her acquaintance with Alfred Stieglitz and met members of his circle, including Paul Strand. Those contacts and her modest debut as an exhibiting artist in New York City awakened O'Keeffe to the possibilities of a career, of success, of making a living as a painter. A creative person can make art anywhere, but usually only cities offer the stimulation of museums, universities, publishers, theaters, and knowledgeable criticism. Not that O'Keeffe grew unhappy as a teacher; on the contrary, she became increasingly fascinated with teaching. Of this period she later recalled, "Pretty soon I got so interested in teaching I wondered why I should be paid for it."[70] Besides, teaching in Texas allowed O'Keeffe the time to work at her own art, while still earning a regular paycheck. New York as yet offered no such guarantees.

Still, she felt the tug of New York drawing her away from Texas. In some ways she had always felt herself a misfit in the Panhandle towns. Periodically at odds with school administrators over curriculum and teacher decorum (O'Keeffe's behavior was thought to be somewhat unconventional in her dress, her refusal to attend church, and her free associations with men), tensions increased after the United States entered World War I in 1917. Supportive of the American position but opposed to excessive militarism and unbridled aggression in any form, O'Keeffe felt herself increasingly isolated from the college community at Canyon. She grew disillusioned and depressed, then fell physically ill when the dangerous influenza epidemic swept the country early in 1918. She received a medical leave from the college and retreated to Waring, near San Antonio, to convalesce with her friend Leah Harris, herself recovering from tuberculosis.[71] Into this physical and emotional malaise, Stieglitz intervened, sending Strand to escort O'Keeffe to New York. With considerable ambivalence, and in a weakened state, O'Keeffe acquiesced. Once there, Stieglitz offered to support her for a year's uninterrupted painting.

For that she was ready. O'Keeffe's years in Texas had been ones of profound artistic discovery in a kind of self-imposed creative exile. There she encountered new forms, fresh sensations, and the freedom to pursue them. And she had grown personally: the Texas years had clarified her values and awakened new, unfettered feelings.

Though she would never return to live in Texas, she had recorded her months there in a series of unforgettable images. Her Texas landscapes— empty of cultural proscriptions, replete with sensory possibilities—speak simultaneously of the place and her responses to it. Here we have focused on her visual images—powerful watercolors and oils that would come to be regarded as among the most innovative of her career. Still other Texas images are recorded in O'Keeffe's own words—in letters that spread themselves over the page as inventively as her Texas paintings. We have already encountered brief passages from those letters; it is appropriate

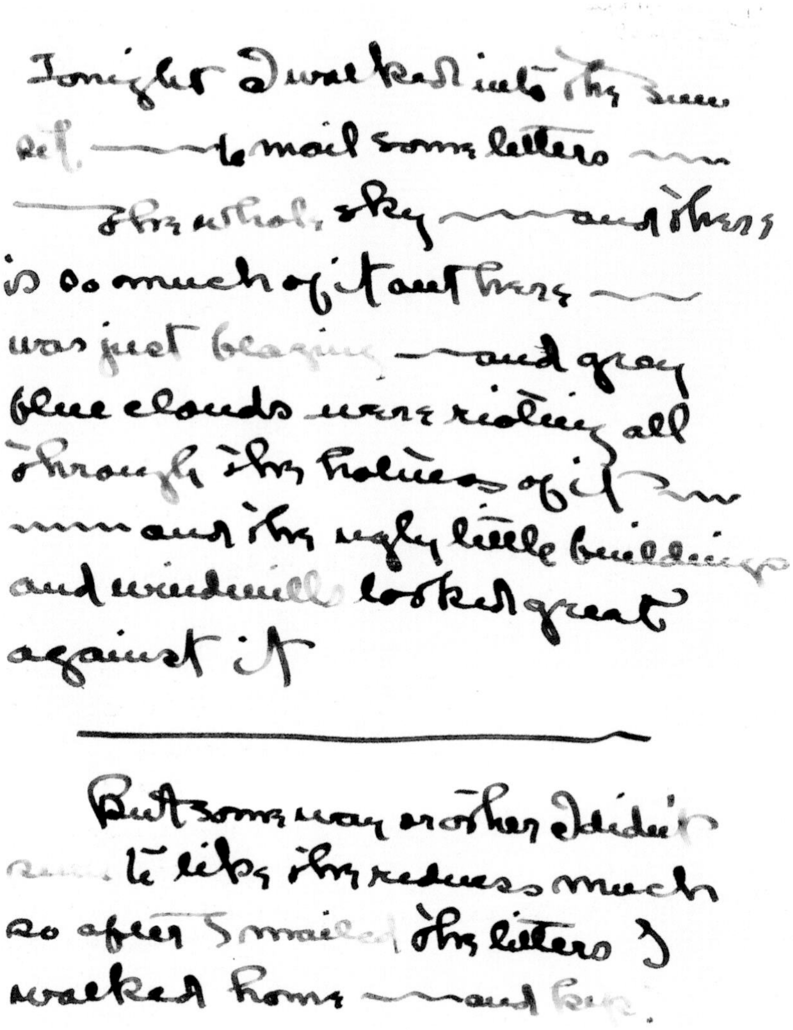

Figure 25
First page of letter written by Georgia
O'Keeffe to Anita Pollitzer from
Canyon, Texas, 11 September 1916
The Yale Collection of American
Literature, Beinecke Rare Book and
Manuscript Library, Yale University

that we acknowledge their collective impact as well.

As a young woman O'Keeffe had developed a keen appreciation for poetry, but when she tried to write verse—rhyming poetry, that is—she failed. What she discovered, it seems, was that she could never be as precise with words as with visual language: "The meaning of a word—to me—is not as exact as the meaning of a color. Colors and shapes make a more definite statement than words."[72] Because she insisted on precision in every aspect of her creative life, O'Keeffe never considered herself much of a writer. Still, there is much we can learn from the Texas letters. Two decades after she left the state, O'Keeffe looked back at some of the letters she had written during those years, recalling "my excitement over the out doors and just being alive—. . . it was like an urge to speak—"[73] When we read those letters now, we hear in them the excitement of discovery. They overflow with every kind of sensation, and with the sense that she was being forever changed by the experience of Texas. In disclosing that deep impact, O'Keeffe conveyed more than she knew.

In another sense—especially as a visual artist—O'Keeffe was right to be suspicious of words and trust her visual vocabulary instead. Words and language are powerful shapers of the world we know. And when used as a linear medium arranged in a time series, language tends to incorporate organizing principles such as causality or historical process. That linearity can convey a false order to the experience of life. Fortunately, O'Keeffe's letters managed to avoid such traps. She thought and wrote in spontaneous, nonlinear fashion. Her holographic layouts in the Texas letters are themselves visually interesting, punctuated by long dashes separating phrases and paragraphs, layered something like those canyon landscapes (see fig. 25). In his book *Cubists and Post-Impressionism*, another text O'Keeffe studied in Texas, Arthur Jerome Eddy argued that conventional punctuation was "too slow" for modern writing; instead, he called for use of the dash as the free vehicle of a terse, substantive style on an unorthodox page.

As if in response to Eddy, O'Keeffe made visual compositions of her words, on pages that complement her paintings. Both forms of expression—writing and painting—demonstrate the modernist's breakdown of artificial barriers of both language and form. On the pages of her letters, for ex-

ample, O'Keeffe would often end a line abruptly, halfway across, then pick it up at another point below, as if to deliberately disrupt time and causality. Sometimes she dropped a thought, then returned to it later in a sentence of new shape. Her visual ambit, both in letters and in her return to painted motifs years after she first put them down, allows us to see vital connections present throughout her work. The patterns traced here—loop processes, interactions, spiraling out and back from core experiences—remind us of the many circular forms in O'Keeffe's paintings. But they also serve as a kind of metaphorical key to O'Keeffe's creativity: in Texas, when the artist often painted things for which she had no words, process overcame subject.

For an artist intent on making an original statement, the expansiveness of West Texas was like a blank page—uncluttered, unspoiled. A decade after O'Keeffe's stay there, D. H. Lawrence discovered some of the same qualities in Texas. For those attuned to it, wrote Lawrence, "It was America, it was Texas. . . . And after all, from the hot wide sky, and the hot, wide, red earth, there *did* come something new, something not used up."[74] O'Keeffe's essential Texas was very much like

Lawrence's. Where other artists might have risked the loss of self in this territory stretching beyond human scale, she embraced its vastness and intensity as means of nurturing and sustaining the self.

In Texas O'Keeffe learned lessons about luminosity and life, about space and spontaneity. She discovered a largeness of sensation that forever drew her back to the vastness of the West. When the East closed in on her, as it often did at Lake George and in Manhattan, the idea of the West held release. Seven years after O'Keeffe's last departure from Texas, Stieglitz, recognizing that longing in her, wrote to a friend, "she dreams of the plains—of real Spaces—. . . . If I were strong enough I guess I'd take her to Texas for a while."[75] Real spaces, after Texas, would always lie under vast open skies that invited O'Keeffe to venture beyond the known, to deepening discoveries of a self in nature.

Notes

1. O'Keeffe, quoted in Calvin Tomkins, "The Rose in the Eye Looked Pretty Fine," *The New Yorker* 50, no. 2 (March 4, 1974), 43.

2. O'Keeffe, letter to Anita Pollitzer, 14 January 1916, quoted in Anita Pollitzer, *A Woman on Paper: Georgia O'Keeffe* (New York: Simon & Schuster, 1988), 126. O'Keeffe's idiosyncratic spelling and punctuation have been preserved here and in subsequent quotations.

3. O'Keeffe, quoted in Roxana Robinson, *Georgia O'Keeffe: A Life* (New York: Harper & Row, 1989), 89.

4. Paul Recer, "Ancient River Ran Through It: Study Explains Rock Finds Across West," *Albuquerque Journal* 5 July 1996, A-2. More of the region's geologic past is discussed in Dan Flores, *Caprock Canyonlands* (Austin: Univ. of Texas Press, 1990), 3–13.

5. O'Keeffe, letter to Anita Pollitzer, 11 September 1916, Yale Collection of American Literature, Beinecke Rare Book and Manuscript Library, Yale University, New Haven (hereafter cited as YCAL).

6. O'Keeffe, quoted in Katharine Kuh, *The Artist's Voice: Talks with Seventeen Artists* (New York: Harper and Row, 1962), 184.

7. O'Keeffe, letter to Anita Pollitzer, 14 January 1916, quoted in Pollitzer, *A Woman on Paper*, 126.

8. Francisco Vazquez de Coronado, quoted in Stewart L. Udall, *To The Inland Empire: Coronado and Our Spanish Legacy* (New York: Doubleday, 1987), 150.

9. Möllhausen, quoted in Martha Doty Freeman, "New Mexico in the Nineteenth Century: The Creation of an Artistic Tradition," *New Mexico Historical Review* 49, no. 1 (January 1974), 16.

10. Thomas Cole, "Essay on American Scenery," quoted in John W. McCoubrey, ed., *American Art 1700–1960: Sources and Documents* (Englewood Cliffs, N.J., 1965), 103. For more on the importance of water in American landscape art, see John Wilmerding, "American Waters: The Flow of Imagination" in John Wilmerding, *American Views: Essays on American Art* (Princeton, N.J.: Princeton Univ. Press, 1991), 49–68.

11. O'Keeffe, quoted in Barbara Haskell, *Arthur Dove* (San Francisco: New York Graphic Society, 1974), 77, 118.

12. O'Keeffe, quoted in Kuh, 190.

13. Arthur Wesley Dow, "Beginnings" [1912] in *Composition: A Series of Exercises in Art Structure for the Use of Students and Teachers* (New York: Doubleday, 1938), 4.

14. O'Keeffe, quoted in Mary Lynn Kotz, "A Day with Georgia O'Keeffe," *ARTnews* 76, no. 10 (December 1977), 43.

15. Ernest Fenollosa, "The Nature of Fine Art," *The Lotos* IX (1896), 759–60.

16. From Dow, *Composition*, 21–28.

17. O'Keeffe, quoted in Tomkins, 64.

18. Arthur W. Dow, letter to Georgia O'Keeffe, 24 April 1917, Stieglitz Collection, YCAL.

19. Dow, letter to O'Keeffe, 18 December 1917, Stieglitz Collection, YCAL.

20. Dow, *Composition*, 50.

21. Dow, quoted in Frederick C. Moffatt, *Arthur Wesley Dow 1857–1922* (Washington, D.C.: Smithsonian Institution Press for the National Collection of Fine Arts, 1977), 117.

22. Dow, quoted in Moffatt, 121.

23. Helmut and Alison Gernsheim, eds. *Alvin Langdon Coburn, Photographer: An Autobiography* (New York: Praeger, 1966), 82–84.

24. O'Keeffe, letter to Anita Pollitzer, possibly 18 September 1916, YCAL. Later, on at least one occasion, O'Keeffe recanted her objections to "prettiness" in art. Interviewed for a 1960 book, she said, "I'm one of the few artists, maybe the only one today, who is willing to talk about my work as pretty. I don't mind it being pretty. I think it's a shame to discard this word; maybe if we work on it hard enough we can make it fashionable again." O'Keeffe, quoted in Kuh, 194.

25. Coronado's party probably experienced the storm passing overhead in nearby Blanco Canyon, rather than Palo Duro.

26. O'Keeffe, letters to Anita Pollitzer, n.d. and 3 October 1916, Stieglitz Collection, YCAL.

27. O'Keeffe, letter to Anita Pollitzer, possibly 18 September 1916, YCAL.

28. O'Keeffe, statement in *Georgia O'Keeffe* (New York: Viking, 1976), opposite plate 5.

29. The Canyon Suite is a group of O'Keeffe's Texas watercolors at the Kemper Museum of Contemporary Art & Design, Kansas City; these paintings were shown simultaneously as a separate exhibition *Georgia O'Keeffe: Canyon Suite* with the *O'Keeffe and Texas* exhibition at the

McNay Art Museum in 1998. For illustrations of the Canyon Suite watercolors not reproduced here, the reader is referred to one of the previously published catalogues of the Canyon Suite (references given in text are to the 1995 book). They are *Georgia O'Keeffe Canyon Suite*, introd. Barbara J. Bloemink (New York: George Braziller and the Kemper Museum of Contemporary Art & Design, Kansas City, 1995); *Georgia O'Keeffe Canyon Suite* (Kansas City: Kemper Museum of Contemporary Art & Design of Kansas City Art Institute, 1994); and *Canyon Suite: Early Watercolors by Georgia O'Keeffe*, afterword Charles C. Eldredge (Santa Fe: The Gerald Peters Gallery and the Kemper Collection, 1994).

30. O'Keeffe, statement in *Georgia O'Keeffe: Some Memories of Drawings*, ed. Doris Bry (Albuquerque: Univ. of New Mexico Press, 1974), n.p.

31. O'Keeffe, statement in *Some Memories of Drawings*, n.p.

32. O'Keeffe, letter to Anita Pollitzer, n.d. [contextually September or October 1916], YCAL.

33. O'Keeffe, letter to Anita Pollitzer, 3 October 1916, YCAL.

34. See Fenollosa, vol. 2, plates following p. 205.

35. O'Keeffe, letter to Alfred Stieglitz, fall 1916, quoted in Pollitzer, *A Woman on Paper*, 148–49.

36. O'Keeffe, letter to Anita Pollitzer, 30 October 1916, YCAL.

37. O'Keeffe, statement in *Georgia O'Keeffe*, opposite plate 46.

38. O'Keeffe, quoted in Tomkins, 54.

39. O'Keeffe, letter to Anita Pollitzer, 21 June 1916, YCAL.

40. O'Keeffe, letter to Anita Pollitzer, 11 September 1916, YCAL.

41. Ernest Fenollosa, "The Nature of Fine Art," quoted in Marianne W. Martin, "Some American Contributions to Early Twentieth-Century Abstraction," *Arts* (June 1980), 159.

42. O'Keeffe, statement in *Georgia O'Keeffe*, opposite plate 6.

43. Ezra Pound, *Gaudier-Brzeska: A Memoir* (London, 1916), cited in Martin, "Some American Contributions to Early Twentieth-Century Abstraction," 159. The similarity of Fenollosa's thoughts to Pound's is no coincidence. In 1915 Pound had published *Cathay*, an important volume of Chinese poems he translated "from the notes of the late Ernest Fenollosa." We do not know whether O'Keeffe directly encountered Pound's writings while she was in Texas, but his work was well known to members of the Stieglitz circle by that time. Marsden Hartley, for example, had met Pound in London in 1912. In the voluminous Stieglitz-O'Keeffe correspondence (begun in 1916, but unavailable to researchers) Stieglitz, who recommended many writers to O'Keeffe, may have discussed such ideas with her.

44. O'Keeffe, letter to Anita Pollitzer, possibly 18 September 1916, YCAL.

45. O'Keeffe, quoted in Tomkins, 43.

46. Norman O. Brown, *Love's Body* (New York: Random House, 1966), 246.

47. Virginia Woolf, from her essay "Modern Fiction" (1919).

48. Dow had staged an exhibition of the art of American school children in London in 1908, and in 1912 Abraham Walkowitz arranged an exhibition of children's art at Stieglitz's Gallery 291.

49. Dow, *Composition*, 23.

50. O'Keeffe, quoted in Tomkins, 42.

51. O'Keeffe, letter to Paul Strand, 3 June 1917, reprinted in Jack Cowart, Juan Hamilton, and Sarah Greenough, *Georgia O'Keeffe: Art and Letters* (Washington: National Gallery of Art, 1987), no. 17, p. 161.

52. O'Keeffe, letter to Paul Strand, 23 July 1917, reprinted in *Georgia O'Keeffe: Art and Letters*, no. 20, pp. 164–65.

53. Eleven years later, in the midst of an intensely energizing first summer in New Mexico, she remarked in a letter to Strand that Taos "is quite as grand as that San Antonio time—" O'Keeffe, to Paul Strand, May 1929, reprinted in *Georgia O'Keeffe: Art and Letters*, no. 45, p. 190.

54. This tiny dot from the lighthouse is unquestionably a formal descendant of the light mote in O'Keeffe's *Black Abstraction* (1917; cat. 19), painted the previous year.

55. O'Keeffe, statement in *Georgia O'Keeffe*, opposite plate 64.

56. O'Keeffe, letter to Elizabeth Stieglitz [Davidson], January 1918, reprinted in *Georgia O'Keeffe: Art and Letters*, no. 23, pp. 166–67.

57. Wassily Kandinsky, *Concerning the Spiritual in Art*, trans. M. T. H. Sadler (1914; reprint, New York: Dover, 1977), 32.

58. This concept—that effective images could be viewed from any side—was

of vital interest to Dow and to photographers such as Paul Strand and Alvin Langdon Coburn, who were studying the possibilities of abstract design in photographs.

59. Bram Dijkstra, ed. *A Recognizable Image: William Carlos Williams on Art and Artists* (New York: New Directions, 1978), 58.

60. O'Keeffe, statement in *Georgia O'Keeffe*, opposite plate 58.

61. O'Keeffe, letter to Anita Pollitzer, n.d. [contextually, late 1916–early 1917], Stieglitz Collection, YCAL.

62. O'Keeffe, statement in *O'Keeffe*, opposite plate 3.

63. The idea was not a new one. The nineteenth-century romantics linked music and painting, while Baudelaire talked of "correspondences" and Wagner's concept of the *gesamtkunstwerk* strove for the union of light and sound. In the 1890s the term *synesthesia* appeared in psychiatric literature, describing sensations generated in one sensory field and perceived in another (such as a sound producing a sensation of color). Subsequently the symbolists, the futurists and, particularly, Wassily Kandinsky carried forth the linkage of color, sound, odors, and moods.

64. O'Keeffe, letter to Anita Pollitzer, 11 September 1916, YCAL.

65. Ted Reid, quoted in Pollitzer, *A Woman on Paper*, 154.

66. O'Keeffe, quoted in Lloyd Goodrich and Doris Bry, *Georgia O'Keeffe* (New York: Whitney Museum of American Art, 1970), 23.

67. Carl Jung, "Introduction to the Religious and Psychological Problems of Alchemy," in *The Basic Writings of C. G. Jung*, trans. R. F. C. Hull (Princeton, N.J.: Princeton Univ. Press, 1990), 476–77.

68. O'Keeffe, statement in *Georgia O'Keeffe*, opposite plate 88.

69. O'Keeffe, statement in *Georgia O'Keeffe*, opposite plate 104.

70. O'Keeffe, quoted in Tomkins, 43.

71. A group of watercolor nudes O'Keeffe painted in Texas may date from this period of convalescence with Leah Harris. Because they remain anomalous in O'Keeffe's work, without the later formal echoes originating so distinctly from her other Texas subjects, the nudes have not been included in this exhibition.

72. O'Keeffe, introductory remark in *Georgia O'Keeffe*, n.p.

73. O'Keeffe, letter to Cady Wells, spring 1939 (?), reprinted in *Georgia O'Keeffe: Art and Letters*, no. 77, p. 227.

74. D. H. Lawrence, *St. Mawr and the Man Who Died* (New York: Vintage, 1925), 129.

75. Alfred Stieglitz, letter to Waldo Frank, 25 August 1925, YCAL.

Sharyn R. Udall

Georgia O'Keeffe: A Chronology

1887
born in Sun Prairie, Wisconsin (November 15), the second child and first girl in a family of seven children

1887–1902
spends early childhood on family's prosperous dairy farm; attends local schools in Sun Prairie and Madison, Wisconsin; receives private art instruction

1902
O'Keeffe family moves to Williamsburg, Virginia

1903
enrolls at Chatham Episcopal Institute, Chatham, Virginia, meets first female mentor, instructor Elizabeth May Willis; graduates 1905

1906
stricken with typhoid, first of many long convalescences during her life

1907
enrolls at Art Students League, New York City; studies with F. Luis Mora, Kenyon Cox, William Merritt Chase; sees exhibitions by Rodin and Matisse at Alfred Stieglitz's Little Galleries of the Photo-Secession (called "291" for its Fifth Avenue address)

1908
attends Art Students League summer school at Lake George, New York

1908–10
works as commercial artist in Chicago drawing lace and advertising logos; returns to live with her family in Charlottesville, Virginia, after measles temporarily weakens her eyes

1911
first experience teaching art, at Chatham Institute

1912
studies with Alon Bement at University of Virginia summer school; begins teaching art for two years in Amarillo, Texas, public schools

1913–16
Summers: teaches art with Alon Bement at University of Virginia summer school

1914–15
studies with Arthur Wesley Dow at Teachers College, Columbia University, New York; sees work of Braque, Picasso, Hartley, and Marin at 291; joins National Woman's Party; meets Anita Pollitzer

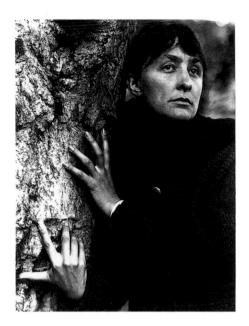

Alfred Stieglitz
Georgia O'Keeffe: A Portrait 1918
Silver gelatin developed-out print
National Gallery of Art, Washington, D.C.,
Alfred Stieglitz Collection

1915
teaches at Columbia College, South Carolina; makes large charcoal abstractions

1916
January: Pollitzer shows O'Keeffe's drawings to Stieglitz; he and O'Keeffe begin corresponding

March–June: O'Keeffe again studies at Teachers College, Columbia University; sees Hartley exhibition at 291

paints *Blue Lines X* (fig. 21), reintroducing color into her work

May: O'Keeffe's mother dies of tuberculosis; first public exhibition of O'Keeffe's drawings and watercolors in group show

September: begins teaching at West Texas State Normal College, Canyon, Texas; paints her first Southwest landscapes

November–December: included with Hartley, Marin, Stanton MacDonald Wright, and Abraham Walkowitz in group show at 291

1917
April: O'Keeffe has her first solo exhibition at Alfred Stieglitz's gallery 291, New York; her charcoal drawing *Train at Night in the Desert* sells for $400, her first sale

April: exhibits two works in Society of Independent Artists exhibition, New York

Early summer: visits New York, meeting members of the Stieglitz circle; Stieglitz photographs her for the first time; in summer, vacations and paints in Colorado, traveling via New Mexico

1918
suffers influenza attack, resigns teaching job in Texas; recuperates in Waring and San Antonio, Texas

June: moves to New York; begins relationship with Stieglitz as protégée, regular photographic model, lover

November: O'Keeffe's father dies

1918–29
O'Keeffe and Stieglitz spend summers at his family's compound at Lake George, New York, winters in New York City

1919
O'Keeffe paints music-inspired abstractions; she and Stieglitz work closely, showing their work privately

1920
O'Keeffe visits York Beach, Maine, alone; she and Stieglitz move into his brother's house on 65th Street, where they live until 1924

1921
Stieglitz exhibits photographs of O'Keeffe at the Anderson Galleries, New York; Marsden Hartley praises her work in sexual terms

1923
O'Keeffe exhibits one hundred works at Anderson Galleries; Stieglitz shows 116 new photographs, including many of O'Keeffe

1924
O'Keeffe and Stieglitz exhibit paintings and photographs simultaneously at Anderson Galleries; O'Keeffe begins large floral, corn, and leaf paintings; O'Keeffe and Stieglitz marry

1925
O'Keeffe and Stieglitz move to Shelton Hotel, New York City, from which she paints her first skyscrapers; Stieglitz opens Intimate Gallery, where O'Keeffe supervises most installations of exhibits, including her own subsequent annual shows

1926
O'Keeffe addresses National Woman's Party, Washington, D.C.; paints East River in pastel and oil; in September begins series of clamshell paintings and pastels while at York Beach, Maine

1927
O'Keeffe undergoes two surgeries for breast lump; slow recovery; paints *Black Abstraction* (cat. 19)

1928
O'Keeffe exhibits fruit and flower paintings in her annual exhibition; travels again to Maine, to visit family in Wisconsin, to Lake George, where Stieglitz suffers a heart attack in September

1929
O'Keeffe spends most of the summer painting at Taos, New Mexico, as guest of Mabel Dodge Luhan; learns to drive and purchases Ford; Stieglitz opens An American Place

1930
O'Keeffe exhibits New Mexico subjects at An American Place

Summer: returns to New Mexico this and most summers until her permanent move there; begins first skeletal subjects

1932
O'Keeffe travels to Gaspe Peninsula in Canada in August; accepts commission for mural in ladies powder room, Radio City Music Hall, but technical problems halt the work; she suffers nervous breakdown, abandons painting for more than a year

1933
February–March: O'Keeffe hospitalized in New York for psychoneurosis, recuperates in Bermuda and Lake George

1934
O'Keeffe has retrospective of forty-four paintings at Stieglitz's gallery; Metropolitan Museum of Art buys a painting; she convalesces in Bermuda, then returns to New Mexico, where she visits Ghost Ranch

1935
annual exhibition includes work from 1919 to 1934; stays at Ghost Ranch June–November

1936
annual exhibition includes all new work from previous summer

Summer: paints at Ghost Ranch

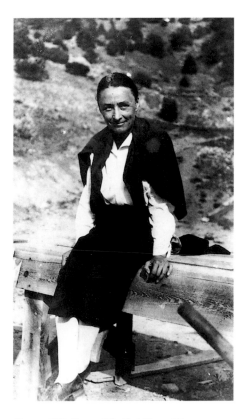

Georgia O'Keeffe near "The Pink House," Taos, New Mexico 1929
Silver gelatin print
Collection of the Museum of New Mexico (negative #9763)

1937

accepts commission for large flower painting at Elizabeth Arden Salon, New York; stays at Ghost Ranch July–December; paints *From the Faraway Nearby*; travels in the West with Ansel Adams and other friends

1938

Stieglitz has another heart attack; O'Keeffe receives honorary doctorate from the College of William and Mary; stays at Ghost Ranch August–November

1939

honored at New York World's Fair as one of twelve outstanding women of past fifty years; paints in Hawaii, later becomes ill and exhausted

1940

buys house at Ghost Ranch, New Mexico, during six-month visit

1941

stays at Ghost Ranch June–December

1942

receives honorary degree from University of Wisconsin, visits family there and in Chicago; campaigns for equal rights amendment; moves with Stieglitz to smaller apartment on 54th Street, New York City

1943

has full scale retrospective at Art Institute of Chicago; begins series based on animal pelvis bones

1944

exhibits pelvis and cottonwood tree subjects in her annual exhibition at An American Place; in New Mexico April–November

1945

acquires ruined adobe house in Abiquiu; with friend Maria Chabot undertakes a three-year restoration project, after which the house becomes O'Keeffe's winter home and studio

1946

O'Keeffe given retrospective at Museum of Modern Art, New York, the first solo show there of a woman's work; begins patio series at Abiquiu, continues it until 1960; Alfred Stieglitz dies in New York at age eighty-two (July 13)

1949

after three years of settling Stieglitz's estate and painting little, O'Keeffe moves permanently to New Mexico and into her renovated adobe house at Abiquiu; O'Keeffe closes An American Place gallery; Edith Halpert's Downtown Gallery becomes her new dealer (until 1963)

1951

visits Mexico, including Yucatán, Oaxaca, and Guadalajara, beginning a decade of international travel

1952

exhibits twenty-four pastels (made 1915–45) at Downtown Gallery

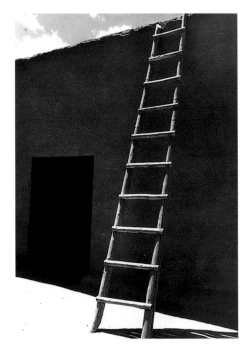

Todd Webb
Ladder and Wall, O'Keeffe's Abiquiu House
1956
Silver gelatin print
Collection of the Museum of Fine Arts,
Museum of New Mexico, Santa Fe,
Todd Webb Study Collection, Gift of
the Artist

1953
makes first trip to Europe (France and Spain)

1954
visits Spain for three months

1956
makes three-month trip to Peru, paints Andean and coastal subjects

1959
travels around the world for three and a half months (India, Japan, Hong Kong, Taiwan, Southeast Asia, Pakistan, the Near East, Rome); observes and begins painting aerial views of rivers

1960
has fourth retrospective exhibition, at Worcester (Massachusetts) Art Museum; takes six-week trip to Asia and the Pacific

1961
makes seven-day raft trip on Colorado River

1962
elected to American Academy of Arts and Letters

1963
travels to Greece, Egypt, and the Near East

1965
paints her largest canvas, *Sky Above Clouds IV*

1966
has retrospective at Amon Carter Museum, Fort Worth; travels to England and Austria

1970
Whitney Museum of American Art, New York, holds major O'Keeffe retrospective

1971
O'Keeffe's vision fails, leaving only peripheral sight

1972
O'Keeffe makes last unassisted painting in oil

1973
O'Keeffe meets and hires Juan Hamilton as assistant; makes hand-built clay pots

1974
O'Keeffe visits Morocco, writes text for *Some Memories of Drawings*

1975
O'Keeffe paints watercolors and assisted oils; Perry Miller Adato produces a documentary film on O'Keeffe and her work

1976
travels to Antigua, publishes her book *Georgia O'Keeffe*

1978
exhibition *Georgia O'Keeffe: A Portrait by Alfred Stieglitz* opens at Metropolitan Museum of Art, New York

1980
Laurie Lisle's unauthorized biography *Portrait of an Artist* published

1982
travels to Hawaii; exhibits large version of her sculpture *Abstraction* at San Francisco Museum of Modern Art

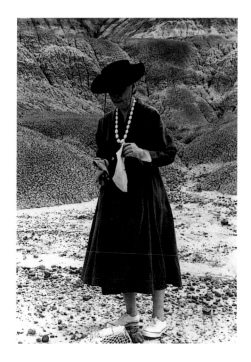

Todd Webb
Georgia O'Keeffe at the Black Place ca.1960
Silver gelatin print
Collection of the Museum of Fine Arts,
Museum of New Mexico, Santa Fe,
Todd Webb Study Collection, Gift of the Artist

1984
moves to Santa Fe to be near medical
services; by now essentially blind

1986
dies in Santa Fe, New Mexico (March 6);
will is challenged by family and state of
New Mexico

1987
major retrospective of O'Keeffe's work
opens at National Gallery of Art, Washington, D.C., with catalogue of her art
and letters

1989
The Georgia O'Keeffe Foundation
established

1997
Georgia O'Keeffe Museum opens in
Santa Fe

Checklist of the Exhibition

Landforms

1.
Special No. 32 1914
Pastel on paper
14 × 19½ in. (35.6 × 49.5 cm)
Collection of the National Museum of
American Art, Smithsonian Institution,
Washington, D.C., Gift of The Georgia
O'Keeffe Foundation

2.
Special No. 9 1915
Charcoal on paper
25 × 19⅛ in. (63.5 × 48.6 cm)
The Menil Collection, Houston

3.
Drawing XIII 1915
Charcoal on paper
24½ × 19 in. (62.2 × 48.3 cm)
The Metropolitan Museum of Art, New
York, Alfred Stieglitz Collection, 1950

4.
Special No. 21 (Palo Duro Canyon) 1916
Oil on canvas
13⅜ × 16⅛ in. (34 × 41 cm)
Collection of the Museum of Fine Arts,
Museum of New Mexico, Santa Fe, Gift
of the Estate of Georgia O'Keeffe

5.
Pink and Green Mountains No. 1 1917
Watercolor on paper
9 × 12 in. (22.9 × 30.5 cm)
Collection of the Spencer Museum of
Art, The University of Kansas,
Lawrence, Letha Churchill Walker Fund

6.
Red Landscape 1918
Oil on board
25 × 19 in. (63.5 × 48.3 cm)
Collection of the Panhandle-Plains His-
torical Museum, Canyon, Texas, Gift of
The Georgia O'Keeffe Foundation

7.
Series 1, No. 1 1918
Oil on board
19¾ × 16 in. (50.2 × 40.6 cm)
Collection of the Amon Carter Museum,
Fort Worth, Purchased in part with funds
provided by the Anne Burnett Tandy
Accessions Fund

8.
Lake George with Crows 1921
Oil on canvas
28⅜ × 24⅞ in. (72 × 63.2 cm)
Collection of the National Gallery of
Canada, Ottawa, Gift of The Georgia
O'Keeffe Foundation

9.
Storm Cloud, Lake George 1923
Oil on canvas
18 × 30 in. (45.7 × 76.2 cm)
Private Collection, Courtesy of
The Gerald Peters Gallery, Santa Fe

10.
Lake George 1924
Oil on canvas
18 × 35 in. (45.7 × 88.9 cm)
Collection of Barbara and James Palmer

11.
Wave, Night 1928
Oil on canvas
30 × 36 in. (76.2 × 91.4 cm)
Collection of the Addison Gallery of
American Art, Phillips Academy,
Andover, Massachusetts, Purchased as
the gift of Charles L. Stillman

12.
Dark Mesa and Pink Sky 1930
Oil on canvas
16¼ × 30⅜ in. (41.3 × 77.2 cm)
Collection of the Amon Carter Museum,
Fort Worth

13.
Untitled (Bear Lake) 1931
Oil on canvas
16½ × 36½ in. (41.9 × 92.7 cm)
Collection of the Museum of Fine Arts,
Museum of New Mexico, Santa Fe,
Museum of New Mexico Foundation

14.
Grey Hills 1942
Oil on canvas
20 × 30 in. (50.8 × 76.2 cm)
Collection of the Indianapolis Museum
of Art, Gift of Mr. and Mrs. James W.
Fesler

Light

15.
Red, Blue and Green 1915
Watercolor on paper
17½ × 13 in. (44.5 × 33 cm)
Collection of the Tobin Foundation

16.
Abstraction Pale Sun 1917
Watercolor
17½ × 13¼ in. (44.5 × 33.7 cm)
Collection of The Gerald Peters Gallery,
Santa Fe

17.
Evening Star, No. V 1917
Watercolor
8⅝ × 11⅝ in. (21.9 × 29.5 cm)
Collection of The McNay Art Museum,
San Antonio, Bequest of Helen Miller
Jones

18.
Red Hills, Lake George 1927
Oil on canvas
27 × 32 in. (68.5 × 81.3 cm)
The Phillips Collection, Washington,
D.C.

19.
Black Abstraction 1927
Oil on canvas
30 × 40¼ in. (76.2 × 102.2 cm)
The Metropolitan Museum of Art, New
York, Alfred Stieglitz Collection, 1969

20.
Jack-in-the-Pulpit VI 1930
Oil on canvas
36 × 18 in. (91.4 × 45.7 cm)
National Gallery of Art, Washington,
D.C., Alfred Stieglitz Collection,
Bequest of Georgia O'Keeffe

Geometric Patterns

21.
Yellow House 1917
Watercolor on paper
9 × 11¾ in. (22.9 × 29.8 cm)
Collection of The Gerald Peters Gallery,
Santa Fe

22.
Roof with Snow 1917
Watercolor on paper
8⅝ × 11¾ in. (21.9 × 29.8 cm)
Collection of the Amarillo Museum
of Art

23.
Roof with Snow—Study Sketch 1917
Watercolor on paper
4 × 5½ in. (10.2 × 14 cm)
Collection of the Amarillo Museum
of Art

24.
Roof with Snow—Study Sketch 1917
Watercolor on paper
4½ × 5½ in. (11.4 × 14 cm)
Collection of the Amarillo Museum
of Art

25.
Abstraction Blue 1917
Watercolor
15¾ × 10⅞ in. (40 × 27.6 cm)
Collection of The Gerald Peters Gallery,
Santa Fe

26.
Window—Red and Blue Sill 1918
Watercolor on paper
11¾ × 8¾ in. (29.8 × 22.2 cm)
Collection of the Georgia O'Keeffe
Museum, Santa Fe, Gift of the Burnett
Foundation

27.
Red Barn, Lake George, New York 1921
Oil on canvas
14 × 16¹⁄₁₆ in. (35.6 × 40.8 cm)
Collection of the Georgia Museum of
Art, University of Georgia, Athens, Eva
Underhill Holbrook Memorial Collec-
tion of American Art, Gift of Alfred H.
Holbrook, GMOA 45.70

28.
Lake George Window 1929
Oil on canvas
40 × 30 in. (101.6 × 76.2 cm)
Collection of The Museum of Modern
Art, New York, Acquired through the
Richard D. Brixey Bequest

29.
Gray Cross with Blue 1929
Oil on canvas
36⅛ × 24⅛ in. (91.8 × 61.3 cm)
Collection of The Albuquerque Mu-
seum, Museum Purchase with funds from
1983–1985 General Obligation Bonds,
The Frederick R. Weisman Foundation,
Ovenwest Corporation, and The Albu-
querque Museum Foundation

30.
From the Patio I 1940
Oil on canvas
24 × 19 in. (61 × 48.3 cm)
Collection of The Gerald Peters Gallery,
Santa Fe

31.
Wall with Green Door 1952
Oil on canvas
30 × 47⅞ in. (76.2 × 121.6 cm)
Collection of The Corcoran Gallery
of Art, Washington, D.C., Gift of the
Woodward Foundation

32.
Sky Above Clouds III 1963
Oil on canvas
48 × 84 in. (121.9 × 213.4 cm)
Private Collection

Solids and Voids

33.
Blue I ca.1917
Watercolor on paper
30¾ × 22⅜ in. (78.1 × 56.8 cm)
Collection of Robert L. B. Tobin

34.
Train Coming In—Canyon, Texas 1918
Watercolor on paper
11⅞ × 8⅞ in. (30.1 × 22.5 cm)
Collection of the Amarillo Museum
of Art

35.
Blue and Green Music 1919
Oil on canvas
23 × 19 in. (58.4 × 48.3 cm)
Collection of The Art Institute of Chi-
cago, Alfred Stieglitz Collection, Gift of
Georgia O'Keeffe

36.
Orange and Red Streak 1919
Oil on canvas
27 × 23 in. (68.6 × 58.4 cm)
Philadelphia Museum of Art, Bequest of
Georgia O'Keeffe for the Alfred Stieglitz
Collection

37.
Leaf Motif #2 1924
Oil on canvas
35 × 18 in. (88.9 × 45.7 cm)
Collection of The McNay Art Museum,
San Antonio, Mary and Sylvan Lang
Collection

38.
Abstraction, Blue 1927
Oil on canvas
40¼ × 30 in. (102.2 × 76.2 cm)
Collection of The Museum of Modern
Art, New York, Acquired through the
Helen Acheson Bequest

39.
Iris (Dark Iris No. 1) 1927
Oil on canvas
32 × 12 in. (81.3 × 30.5 cm)
Collection of the Colorado Springs Fine
Arts Center

40.
Pink Abstraction 1929
Oil on canvas
36 × 30 in. (91.4 × 76.2 cm)
Collection of the Phoenix Art Museum,
Gift of Friends of Art

41.
Red Hills with White Shell 1938
Oil on canvas
30 × 36½ in. (76.2 × 92.7 cm)
Collection of The Museum of Fine Arts,
Houston, Gift of Isabel Wilson in
memory of her mother, Alice Pratt
Brown

42.
Pelvis with Blue (Pelvis I) 1944
Oil on canvas
36 × 30 in. (91.4 × 76.2 cm)
Collection of the Milwaukee Art Mu-
seum, Gift of Mrs. Harry Lynde Bradley

43.
Abstraction 1945, cast 1980
White lacquered bronze
36 in. high (91.4 cm)
Collection of The Gerald Peters Gallery,
Santa Fe

44.
From the Plains I 1953
Oil on canvas
47¹¹⁄₁₆ × 83⅝ in. (121.1 × 212.4 cm)
Collection of The McNay Art Museum,
San Antonio, Gift of the Estate of Tom
Slick

45.
Blue I 1958
Oil on canvas
30⅛ × 26⅛ in. (76.5 × 66.4 cm)
Collection of The Snite Museum of Art,
University of Notre Dame, Gift of Mr.
Walter Beardsley

50.
From the River—Light Blue 1964
Oil on canvas
40 × 30 in. (101.6 × 76.2 cm)
Collection of the Museum of Fine Arts,
Museum of New Mexico, Santa Fe, Gift
of the Estate of Georgia O'Keeffe

Lines

46.
Dark Abstraction 1924
Oil on canvas
24⅞ × 20⅞ in. (63.2 × 53 cm)
Collection of The Saint Louis Art
Museum, Gift of Charles E. and Mary
Merrill

47.
It Was Yellow and Pink II 1959
Oil on canvas
36 × 30 in. (91.4 × 76.2 cm)
Collection of The Cleveland Museum
of Art, Bequest of Georgia O'Keeffe

48.
Winter Road I 1963
Oil on canvas
22¹⁄₁₆ × 18⅛ in. (56 × 46 cm)
Collection of the National Gallery of
Art, Washington, D.C., Gift of The
Georgia O'Keeffe Foundation

49.
Road Past the View 1964
Oil on canvas
18 × 30 in. (45.7 × 76.2 cm)
Private Collection

Lenders to the Exhibition

Albuquerque
The Albuquerque Museum

Amarillo
Amarillo Museum of Art

Andover, Massachusetts
Addison Gallery of American Art,
  Phillips Academy

Athens, Georgia
Georgia Museum of Art, University of
  Georgia

Canyon, Texas
Panhandle-Plains Historical Museum

Chicago
The Art Institute of Chicago

Cleveland
The Cleveland Museum of Art

Colorado Springs
Colorado Springs Fine Arts Center

Dallas
Private Collection

Fort Worth
Amon Carter Museum

Houston
The Menil Collection
The Museum of Fine Arts, Houston

Indianapolis
Indianapolis Museum of Art
Private Collection

Lawrence, Kansas
Spencer Museum of Art, The University
  of Kansas

Milwaukee
Milwaukee Art Museum

New York
The Metropolitan Museum of Art
The Museum of Modern Art

Notre Dame, Indiana
The Snite Museum of Art, University of
  Notre Dame

Ottawa
National Gallery of Canada

Philadelphia
Philadelphia Museum of Art

Phoenix
Phoenix Art Museum

Saint Louis
The Saint Louis Art Museum

San Antonio
The McNay Art Museum
Robert L. B. Tobin
Tobin Foundation

Santa Fe
Georgia O'Keeffe Museum
The Gerald Peters Gallery
Museum of Fine Arts, Museum of
  New Mexico

State College, Pennsylvania
Barbara and James Palmer

Washington, D.C.
The Corcoran Gallery of Art
National Gallery of Art
National Museum of American Art,
  Smithsonian Institution
The Phillips Collection

Board of Trustees, The McNay Art Museum

Trustees

Mr. Robert L. B. Tobin
Chairman

Mr. Thomas R. Semmes
President

Mr. Charles E. Foster
Vice President

Ms. Alice C. Simkins
Secretary

Mr. Allan G. Paterson
Treasurer

Mrs. Michael Baucum

Mrs. William J. Block

Mr. Jonathan C. Calvert

Mr. E. H. Corrigan

Mr. George H. Ensley

Mr. Thomas C. Frost

Mrs. Hugh Halff

Mr. Walter Nold Mathis

Mrs. B. J. McCombs

Mr. Jesse H. Oppenheimer

Mr. Michael J. C. Roth

Mrs. Arthur Stieren

Mr. W. Lawrence Walker

Mr. Harold J. Wood

Honorary Trustees

Mr. Robert Halff

Mrs. Nancy B. Hamon

Mrs. Nancy Brown Wellin

Emeritus Trustees

Mr. Walter F. Brown

Mrs. George J. Condos

Mr. George C. Hixon

Mrs. H. T. Johnson

Mrs. Irving Mathews

Mrs. Ethel T. Runion

Mr. Gaines Voigt

Advisory Trustee

Mr. William A. Jeffers, Jr.
President, Friends of The McNay

0000112512058

Photograph Credits

Fig. 2: © Wyman Meinzer

Fig. 4: Photo by Bill Lane

Figs. 7, 20: © 1997 Board of Trustees, National Gallery of Art

Figs. 10, 11: © Georgia O'Keeffe Museum

Fig. 15: © 1971 Aperture Foundation Inc., Paul Strand Archive

Fig. 21: Photo by Malcolm Varon; © 1987 The Metropolitan Museum of Art

Fig. 22: Photo by Lee Ewing; © 1997 Board of Trustees, National Gallery of Art

Cats. 2, 4: © 1987 Malcolm Varon, NYC

Cat. 3: © 1997 The Metropolitan Museum of Art

Cats. 7, 12: © Amon Carter Museum, Fort Worth, Texas

Cats. 9, 21, 30, 43: © The Georgia O'Keeffe Foundation

Cat. 11: © Addison Gallery of American Art, Phillips Academy, Andover, Massachusetts. All Rights Reserved.

Cats. 15, 17, 33, 37, 44: Photos by Michael Jay Smith

Cats. 16, 25: © The Gerald Peters Gallery, Santa Fe

Cat. 19: © 1988 The Metropolitan Museum of Art

Cat. 20: Photo by Richard Carafelli; © 1997 Board of Trustees, National Gallery of Art

Cats. 22, 23, 24, 29: Photos by Damian Andrus

Cat. 26: © Georgia O'Keeffe Museum

Cat. 27: Photo by Michael McKelvey

Cats. 28, 38: © 1997 The Museum of Modern Art, New York

Cat. 35: © 1996 The Art Institute of Chicago. All Rights Reserved.

Cat. 40: Photo by Craig Smith

Cat. 42: Photo by Efraim Lev-er

Cat. 47: © 1997 The Cleveland Museum of Art

Cat. 48: © 1997 Board of Trustees, National Gallery of Art

Page 108: © 1997 Board of Trustees, National Gallery of Art

Pages 110, 111: © Todd Webb

Copyedited by Jessica Eber

Designed by Susan E. Kelly

Produced by Marquand Books, Inc., Seattle

Printed and bound by C & C Offset Printing Co., Ltd.,
    Hong Kong

Typeset in Linotype-Hell Weiss with heads in Agfa Arta